STORIES FOR REFLECTION

Jack McArdle ss.cc.

Stories for
Reflection

the columba press

First published in 1996 by
the columba press
55A Spruce Avenue, Stillorgan Industrial Park,
Blackrock, Co Dublin

Cover by Bill Bolger
Origination by The Columba Press
Printed in Ireland by Colour Books Ltd, Dublin

ISBN 1 85607 172 3

Acknowledgements
I would like to acknowledge with gratitude the friends and col-
leagues who generously read the manuscript. Their observations
have been a great help and encouragement.

Contents

Introduction

Some years ago I wrote a book called *150 Stories for Preachers and Teachers*, followed by *150 More Stories for Preachers and Teachers*. Both books are out of print, and I have no desire to re-issue them. Instead, I have selected some of the best of those stories, added some new ones, to make up the present collection of forty. This time I have done with the stories what I had always wished to do, if time had permitted. I have surrounded and wrapped each story in reflection and simple teaching. I do not accept that just anybody can tell a story! Jesus was a superb storyteller, and he used stories extensively in proclaiming his message. Stories generally are about things with which people are familiar, and this is the spring-board to launch them into less familiar truths.

I have enjoyed writing these reflections. I wrote them primarily for myself, as part of my own quiet times. I believe that a life without reflection is not worth living. These reflections are nothing more than the thoughts and musings of an individual, and, hopefully, in the process, they are given something by God's Spirit that they never could have of themselves. It is with the hope of the Spirit continuing to empower them as sparks of enlightenment and inspiration, that I dare offer them to anyone else. Certainly if the reader gets even a fraction of the blessings in the reading that I received in the writing, then I will consider this work to be truly and doubly blessed.

Because these are some of my own reflections over a period of time, I notice that some thoughts and ideas are repeated in different reflections. For editorial purposes, I could correct this, but it would tend to be artificial, because, obviously, in the normal course of thinking, reflecting, and considering, we all find ourselves returning to the same idea on more than one occasion. I have judged it worthwhile to allow the repetition, which is quite infrequent, actually, because the ideas involved require and deserve to be repeated. Because this book is not intended to belong to the shelves of academia in a library, I have quoted scripture, and, in most cases, I deliberately omitted references to source. In these reflections, I have tended to write exactly the way I speak! Please consider the short prayers at the end of each reflection as being very brief samples of prayers I myself would probably say by way of response. They are included as suggestions, and if they help kick-start another person into praying, then they will have served their purpose.

These reflections are intended for general consumption in a general way. In other words, the reader can open the book at the last chapter! They have no particular order or priority. They can even be a one-a-day dose for those who wish. I hope and expect, however, that my previous readers, the preachers and teachers, may find this book a very useful and helpful resource. Because of them, I can permit the dream of something I have worked with, growing beyond any hopes I might have had, and becoming a potential for speaking gospel truths in a way I never could have envisaged. May the Lord bless all who take over where I have left off.

1. Being sure of acceptance

There is no particular order to these stories. This first one, however, is a deliberate choice to be at number one. It is more of an incident, than a story, but it has the advantage of being something that I, myself, experienced, and it was an incident that made a profound impression on me.

The Gospels can be summarised in one sentence, 'God loves me', and in one word 'Abba', daddy, or Father. If I were to die right now, it is possible that Jesus could ask me a very simple, and basic, question 'Did you come to really believe that my Father loves you?' If I were to express any surprise at the question, Jesus could very well say 'That, in summary, is why I came. In my own life, I lived in the sure and certain knowledge of my Father's love, and, at the Last Supper, I prayed that you would come to know that he loves you as much as he loves me.' Knowledge of God's love must be experiential, and not just academic knowledge. The shepherds were told the good news by angels, which is fairly solid authority, and, yet, they said 'Let us go to Bethlehem to see this thing that has been announced to us by the Lord.' In other words, we have to come into our own personal knowledge of the truth, and no longer believe it just because someone else told us. Acting on the word of another is to act out of belief, while acting out of my own experience is acting on faith. You want your car serviced, and you ask me to recommend a garage. I tell you that I have found Murtagh's to be very reliable, and reasonably priced. You bring your car there, on my word, and you act on belief. Your car is serviced, you are pleased with the job, and the price is reasonable. The next time you need your car serviced, you will return to Murtagh's, but this time you will be acting on faith, because you yourself now know, through personal experience, what you had originally heard from me. The woman at the well brought out all her friends to meet Jesus, and, when they had met him, they told her 'Now we believe, but not because you told us, but because we have met him ourselves.'

'In this is love', says St John. 'Not that we love God, but that he first loved us.' St John tells us that 'God is love', and, therefore, to have any openness to God in our lives, is to be open to his love. In a book called 'As Bread that is Broken', we are told that faith is having the courage to accept God's acceptance of us. The whole story is about something that was put in motion by God. In other words, it is the divine initiative, and it must never be turned into human endeavour. Not to set limits to God's love for me, and to be humble enough to accept his love, unearned and unmerited as it is, is the very essence of holiness. In practice, this means that the saint is not somebody who loves God, but, rather somebody who is convinced that God loves her.

Which brings me to my encounter with Annie. She was in a hospice situation, and she was dying with cancer. She was a simple soul, and her concept of God was simple, direct, and uncomplicated. She was nothing of an intellectual, and she would not at all be into debating, discussing, or arguing religious topics, something that she saw as beyond her. For me, she represented the people Jesus had in mind when he prayed 'Father, I thank you, Lord of heaven and earth, for you have hidden these things from the wise and learned, and made them known to little children.' Annie had the heart of a child, especially when it came to her acceptance of, and her trust in God. If God had chosen to let her have cancer, then she could accept that, because, if it came from God, it could not be bad. I could imagine an intellectual, who lives in his head, having some serious problems with Annie's simplicity!

Anyhow, as time went by, Annie suffered the ravages of a very virulent form of cancer, and was reduced to a mere skeleton, completely jaundiced, even to where the whites of her eyes were yellow. I had the unique privilege of celebrating Eucharist with, and for Annie, and a few of her friends, every afternoon over the last weeks of her life. It was, indeed, a source of great blessing for me, personally, because Annie's faith was so simple that she was profoundly in awe at the privilege that she had, of having Mass celebrated by her bedside every day. I always gave some short reflection on the gospel, and it was a source of quiet humour, while being deeply edifying, when Annie kept interrupting me, to agree fully with everything I was saying! 'That's right, Father, I agree with you! That's what I believe myself.'

Eventually, it was evident that Annie was running out of time. I was with her on a Friday afternoon. I had to travel some distance to give a weekend Retreat, and I was reasonably sure that Annie would not be here when I returned on Monday. I was holding her hands, and praying with her. I gave her absolution 'for everything you ever did wrong, and for all the things you hadn't time to do'! Annie really enjoyed that! I even suggested that maybe, now she was feeling sorry she hadn't done them! I blessed her with oil, and, still holding her hands, I said 'Annie, love, Jesus might come looking for you over the weekend, while I'm away. If he does, please know that your bags are packed, and you're all ready to go.' I then asked her the BIG question 'Do you think you'll be afraid to meet him?', to which she replied, with total conviction 'Father, I'm sure he'll be really glad to see me.' Annie was called home to heaven that night.

I hope that you, dear reader, can see why I wanted to tell Annie's story right at the beginning of this collection. With all the many times we are asked to say 'Yes' in life, the final 'Yes' in death is the greatest of all. Mary said 'Yes', and she left the rest to God. She was told that, following her 'Yes', the Holy Spirit would be with her, and the power of the Most High would over-shadow her. I am more and more convinced that, as life goes on, my prayer can gradually be reduced to a simple 'Yes', and leave the rest to God. At the time of writing, I get to spend a lot of time in the company of those in ongoing care. Every opportunity I get I remind them that 'if it's one walking stick, two walking sticks, a walking aid, or a wheelchair,... just try to say 'yes', and leave the rest to God.' I honestly believe that this is a very real preparation for that great and eternal 'yes' at the end.

Jesus asked 'What does it profit a person, if he gain the whole world, and suffer the loss of his own soul?' Annie had very little of what this world offers, money, education, or social standing. Yet, in the final analysis, she remains, for me, one of the most unique human beings I have ever had the privilege of knowing. When push comes to pull, the acid test is how ready we are when the Lord calls us home. St Paul tells us our salvation is brought about by Christ's blood, and our faith. In other words, it's what Jesus has done, and whether I believe that or not. I don't believe God will send me anywhere when I die. Rather will he eternalise the direction of my life right now. Knowing Annie during those final weeks helped me understand the depth of sincerity contained in her final simple words 'Father, I'm sure he'll be really glad to see me.'

Heavenly, Father, you sent Jesus to tell us that you love us. Through him, you invite us to come back to you, and to be sure of your welcome and your hug. I pray that your Spirit may reveal the fulness of this truth to my heart, so that I can live in that love, and look forward to dying in that love. Thank you for always being there for me, even when I forget you. Thank you, already, for being there to welcome me when I move on to the third and final stage of life. Please help me to long for that moment with some of the longing that you experience. Amen.

2. Jesus as one like us

The whole story of our salvation is based on what is called INCARN-ATION. It is *absolutely vital* that I clearly understand exactly what that means. I live in a body, so I am an incarnate. When I die, and I leave the body, I will be a discarnate. When God, in Jesus, took on a body, and came among us, we say that he became incarnate. Incarnation is about God joining the human race, taking a body like ours, and travelling the journey with us. It is as if he unscrewed the top of our heads, so that he could look out through our eyes, and see things as we see them. In sharing our struggle, he could speak our language.

It is vital that I reflect at great length on this central issue. He that was without sin became sin. He joined us in the struggle, so that he could cry with us, experience the pains, the hungers, and the rejec-tions that we experience. He could have loved us from a distance, but he chose not to. Incarnation is surely the greatest love story ever told. Love, real love, involves going to where another is, and accepting that person as he is. Father Damien goes to the lepers in Molokai, and Mother Teresa goes to the poor and homeless in the slums. Love does not expect the other to earn or merit acceptance, and when we speak of gift, that implies that all price tags are removed from the goods that are offered.

The language of love does not require words. It is a language of the heart, where the Spirit of God lives. That Spirit comes out in all that I do, and in all that I say. Jesus speaks of power leaving him, when the little woman in the crowd touched the hem of his garment. It was as if he were charged with some sort of electric power, that energised all he said and did. I am called to be a channel of that power, but never a generator; to be God's touch-person in the lives of others. I do that when I speak the language of love, when I try to enter into the other person's pain, when I try to be compassionate, as my heavenly Father is compassionate. Compassion literally means to share the pain of another.

One Christmas Eve, a man was wondering why God chose to come on earth as a helpless baby, when, coming in full power and glory would have attracted so much more attention. As he was thinking about this, he heard some commotion out in his backyard, which, at that time of year, was under several feet of snow. He looked out the window, and saw that four green geese had landed in the snow. It seems that they were on their way from the North Pole to the Gulf of Mexico, as part of a larger flock, when one of their number became ill, and was forced to land. As is the instinct with the green geese, three other members dropped out of the formation, to stay with the injured goose. What the man saw were four geese sinking into the soft snow, completely unable to get a firm standing. Being a man of sensitivity and compassion, he immediately wanted to help. He thought that, if he could get them to go into a shed in his back garden, he could phone some agency involved with the welfare of such wildlife, and get help in arranging their safe passage to their destination. He went out into the garden, opened the door of the shed, and tried to direct them towards the open door. His appearance brought complete panic among the geese. They flapped their wings, sunk further into the soft snow, and were in danger of suffocation. He was genuinely concerned for their safety, and he did all he could to move them towards the shed, but all to no avail. He experienced a complete sense of helplessness, and was in despair of being able to help. Just then he had the crazy idea that he wished, with all his heart, that he were a goose! That way, he could speak their language, and tell them, quite simply, what his intentions were, and how much he wanted to help them. Like a bolt from the blue, it dawned on him why Jesus came the way he did! By becoming one of us, 'like us in all things, but sin', he could speak our language, and help us to see that he was on our side, and that his only wish was to help, and to do for us what we could never do for ourselves.

Love is to meet and accept another as that person is, where that person is at. As I said in the commentary leading into the story, just as

Father Damien went to the lepers of Molokai, or Mother Teresa goes into the slums of Calcutta, love goes to where the other person is. St Peter had a problem with this! When Jesus knelt at his feet, with a basin of water and a towel, fully prepared, through the washing of his feet, to accept him at ground level, Peter said 'Lord, you shall never wash my feet.' In those times, it was the task of slaves to wash the feet of those they served. Jesus put a towel around his waist, and was actually dressed like a slave of those times, and this gesture shocked Peter. Jesus insisted, however, on Peter accepting such an expression of love and acceptance. 'If I cannot wash your feet, you cannot be my disciple', he said. Peter, always deeply aware of his own fumbling imperfections, was enough in tune with the person that Jesus was to throw open his heart, and to exclaim 'Lord, not only my feet, but my head and hands as well.' In other words, Peter was prepared to let Jesus love him his way, and submit to the power of such love and acceptance. Faith has been described as the courage to accept God's acceptance. It is difficult, if not impossible, for Jesus to become incarnate in the lives of some people! With the best will in the world, they keep pushing him back up into the sky, while they insist on saving their own souls, as if to say 'Thanks, Jesus, but I would be happier if you stayed where you are, and let me work my way towards you'!! For such people, heaven is seen as a reward for their efforts, and, at the end of the journey, they expect Jesus to pin a medal on them, and to say 'Well done! You deserve the reward of being with me for all eternity.' The problem with that is, that it rejects the love of God, which is called INCARNATION. The saint is not the person who loves God, but the person who is totally convinced that God loves her/him. 'God is love', says John, 'and in this is love, not that we love God, but that he has first loved us.'

One of the greatest paradoxes of Christianity is the power that accompanies littleness. Jesus could have come with heavenly glory, and with all his divine power on display. However, when he came as a helpless baby, he caused terror to rise in the hearts of the Herods of this world. Jesus would later state that the meek shall possess the earth. There is a power in littleness that the world cannot deal with. Ghandi or Martin Luther King refused to meet violence with violence, and the world just had to shoot them, because they could not be stopped in any other way. Coming among us as a helpless baby is a message from Jesus about a very important truth, a truth that merits much prayer and reflection. To understand this truth is to get a very real insight into the mind of Jesus. Satan is a bully, and what must have been a bitter pill to swallow was to have to accept the fact that, with God, strength comes from truth and integrity, and is not a physical thing. 'My strength is as the strength of ten, because my heart is pure', is a saying that merits reflection.

Lord Jesus, how can we ever thank you for what you have done, in coming down to join us just as we are? You came to speak the language of love, and that is a language we all know, even if we don't hear it spoken often enough. Spirit of God, I trust you to reveal such extraordinary love to me, and please help me listen to that language of God in my heart every day. Amen.

3. The Christian witness

Christianity is about attracting, rather than promoting. As a Christian, it is what I am is my message, rather than anything I say. If I enter your house, telling you I have measles, when, in fact, I actually have chicken-pox, which are you liable to catch?! The Gospel is in between two sentences. At the beginning Jesus says 'Come and see', and at the end he says 'Go and tell'. No point in going to tell if I myself never actually came to see for myself. If I am involved in evangelising, it is only because I myself have been evangelised. On Christmas night, the shepherds were told the message by angels (which is fairly reliable testimony!), and yet they said 'Let us go to Bethlehem to see for ourselves this thing which the Lord has made known to us.' I cannot speak with any conviction of anything that is outside my own sphere of experience. I can expound on theories, of course, and those theories can be very sound, but, unless I have personal experience, there will always be something missing in what I am presenting. I do not have to have cancer to speak about it, or to treat it, but, if I do have cancer, I am speaking with a totally different emphasis, and with the depth of experiential knowledge. I am speaking of something I know, not just something I believe. Witnessing must always have some of the quality of experiential knowledge about it.

Christianity is about witnessing. 'You shall be my witnesses to the ends of the earth', says Jesus. In another place, he asks 'Who do you say that I am?' Much more than accepting, believing, or preaching the Gospel, I am asked to live it. 'You write a new page of the Gospel each day, by the things that you do, and the words that you say. People read what you write, whether faithful or true; – what is the Gospel according to you?' You may be the only gospel some people may ever read, because they might never buy the book. I spent a few years working in a parish, a young parish, made up

mostly of young families. As might be expected, the parish had the
usual percentage of non-Church-going people. Again and again I
stressed, in church, that those people were not causing me any concern at all. I believed strongly that, those of us who came to church,
had a serious responsibility to give a very positive witness to the
value of our own church-going. Once that witness became strong
enough, and evident enough, the others would be more open to join
us, because they couldn't deny the evidence of their own senses.

> Some years ago, a missionary in Africa came across the follow-
> ing situation. A whole tribe was preparing for Baptism. The mis-
> sionary was puzzled by the fact that the only exception was the
> old chief of the tribe, who declared, very definitely, that this was
> not for him. The priest didn't push the issue, and, after some
> time, had completely forgotten about it. About three years later,
> he was really surprised when the chief approached him, and
> announced that now he was ready to ask for Baptism. The priest
> readily agreed, but, more out of curiosity than anything else, he
> asked the chief why he had held off until now, and why he had
> refused to be baptised with the rest of his tribe. The chief's
> answer was very simple, very sincere, and very wise. 'All my
> life,' he said, 'I have tried to act wisely. I just could not accept
> Baptism because you, or anyone else suggested it. I needed to
> come to that decision myself. I held back when the rest of my
> tribe were being baptised, and, since that time, I have watched
> them very closely. I needed to see for myself, and to be con-
> vinced by the evidence, that Baptism made a difference in their
> lives. I have seen all the evidence and witness I need, and now I
> am anxious to join them.'

Before Jesus left his apostles to ascend to the throne of his Father,
with his work now completed, he told them 'Very soon now, you
will receive power from on high, and you will become my witnesses.'
In other words, if you accept the privilege, you must also accept the
responsibility. St Paul reminds us that we are ambassadors for
Christ, and, as we speak on his behalf, Jesus asks 'Who do you say
that I am?' It is part of the whole condition of being Christian that I
give witness to the presence of the Spirit in my heart. 'Lord, may
your Spirit within me touch the hearts of those I meet today, either
through the words I say, the prayers I pray, the life I live, or the very

person that I am.' If, as a Christian, I believe that 'I live now, not I, but Christ lives in me', then, surely that inner presence must touch all that I do, and be evident in how I live my life. Witnessing is central to being Christian. I would make a clear distinction between witnessing and evangelising. Not everybody is called to be an evangelist, but we are all called to witness. Witness is an almost unconscious act, because everything I do and say can give witness to Christ's presence within. I could preach a powerful sermon on the gospel, even if I were deaf and dumb.

There are two references in the account of the Last Supper to which I would like to draw attention. The first is where Jesus tells the apostles that others will know they belong to him by the way they love one another. The second is where he prays to the Father that his disciples might be one, so that the world would then believe that Jesus had actually come from God. There is a certain sadness in this, in that Jesus makes himself very vulnerable, when he entrusts the proof of the authenticity of his mission to the witness of our lives. In a way, he puts himself at our mercy, because we can so damage his message, that it is no longer credible.

Have you ever heard the expression 'Get off my back'? and yet Jesus is more or less saying 'Come to me. Get on my back. I will carry you.' These are lines from a song that was made popular a few years ago by a British rock group called The Hollies: 'I'm strong, strong enough to carry him. He ain't heavy, he's my brother.' A Christian, in the words of St Peter, always has an explanation to give to those who ask the reason for the hope that he has. The only real sin for a Christian is to lose hope, and to give up. I would go so far as to say that, in today's world, the witness of hope is just as important as the witness of love. The world needs hope today, because the doomsday prophets never had it so good! With the communications explosion, we are kept well informed about every evil and disaster around the world. This is not a bad thing, but it can effect how we think and look at life. Human nature hasn't undergone any great transformation over the years, either for good or for evil, no matter how we try to analyse it. Abraham Lincoln tried to get someone to be more in touch with reality, when he asked the question 'How many legs would a sheep have if I pretended its tail was a leg?' 'Five' was the answered. 'No', said

Lincoln, 'the sheep would still only have four legs. Pretending the tail is a leg doesn't make it a leg!'

Lord, in calling us to belong in your kingdom, you wish that we would be witnesses to the presence and reality of that kingdom. In thanking you for the call, all I can do is offer you all that I am, so that, your Spirit working in and through me, may give witness that I belong to you. I offer you my good-will, and I trust your Spirit to take it from there. Thank you, Lord. Amen.

4. The source of our problems

When we speak of sin, it is important to remember where sin came from! THE sin is original sin, which is something that was committed against me. It is something of which I am the victim. Because of that I am irreparably damaged, and only God, who created me in the first place, can now recreate me, and make all things new again. Because of that sin I have a hole in the ozone layer of my spirit, as it were, and it is totally beyond me, or all human effort put together, to 'fix' it. God is creator, and only God can do God-things, like recreating. God is not into wall-papering over the cracks. All the dry-rot must be located and rooted out. I sometimes think of the process of redemption going on within, as involving a huge skip for the disposal of the waste and the rubbish that must be gotten rid of, before the Spirit of God can make all things new again. If I use the idea of a heart transplant, I may get a clearer idea of what's involved here. Firstly, the old heart must be diagnosed as no longer capable of preserving life. Then another heart must be procured, and the twin-operation of removing one and implanting the other must be simultaneous. This is major surgery, and, hopefully, when successful, will give a whole new lease of life to the recipient. This is fundamental surgery, because it is getting behind the pains, the lack of energy, the shortage of breath, and it is dealing directly and radically with the problem underlying the condition.

It would be a very poor doctor who would treat symptoms. He would check out the symptoms, to see what the problem is, and treat that. Quite often, my sins are but symptoms of my condition. A sinner committing sin should cause no great surprise. Sin is often more about attitude than about act. Just as one generous act does not make me a generous person, so one selfish act should not have me labelled as a selfish person. Is it possible that, behind all the struggle and failure, there is some deep-rooted problem, that must be discovered, uncovered, named, claimed, and tamed, before I really begin to live? I remember, as a young lad, growing up in the country, being sent by my father to pull thistles, and what we called rag-weeds. After a while, the effort would get too much for me, and progress was too slow for my liking, so I would take a stick and cut the heads off the thistles and the weeds. The problem, of course, was that the thistles grew again, and, once again, I was sent out to repeat the procedure! It is a wise saying that 'When all else fails, try the truth; it always works!'

While conducting Retreats over the years, I often joked about those people who used the time of Retreat as an opportunity to shift around the furniture of their spiritual lives, to re-arrange priorities, and to re-negotiate emphases. This is all very well, except, of course, when the reality called for the whole junk to be thrown in a skip, and to start with a clean slate! One of my earliest memories, as a child, was the special thrill I got when we moved a bed to another part of a bedroom. For a day or two, it was like a whole new bed-room! Similarly with the person on the Retreat. For the brief period of euphoria it is 'Glory be to the Father, to the Son, and to the Holy Spirit', and then, after a certain length of time it is 'As it was in the beginning, is now, and ever shall be.!' In other words, there's really no change. The Gospel is radical, a word than comes from the Latin for 'root'. God is not interested in cutting the head off thistles! 'I make all things new...'.

A man went to a doctor one time, because he was deeply worried. He told the doctor that every part of his body he touched was very very sore to the touch. He used the index finger of his right hand to touch his nose, and that was very painful. The same happened when he touched his elbow, his forehead, or his chin. He was genuinely worried, and he begged the doctor to please find out what was the matter with him. The doctor proceeded to give him a thorough physical examination, which lasted over half an hour. Eventually the doctor was finished, and there was a silence, as the man asked, nervously, 'Well, doctor, did you find out what's wrong with me?' 'I did', said the doctor. 'What's wrong with you is that your right index finger is broken'!

It is often easier to see this kind of thing in the life of an alcoholic. For years, he was convinced that everyone around him was wrong, and he had no end of people and things to blame for how he was, and how he was behaving. Hopefully, some day it dawns on him where and what the problem is. 'My finger is broken' translates, in his case, into 'I am an alcoholic'. Guilt is not from God. In the last book of the Bible (Revelations), Chapter 12, Satan is called 'the accuser of the brothers. He accuses them day and night before our God.' Jesus said that he came to save the world, not to condemn it, and he told the woman, whom the Pharisees were going to stone to death 'Neither do I condemn you. Go in peace ...'. It is very important that I have a clear grasp of the implications of original sin in my life; otherwise, I'm going to spend my life flogging myself to death with guilt, and self-condemnation. I am not making excuses for self-ishness in my life, because much of it can be wilful, and inexcusable. What I speak of here has more to do with drives, addictions, compulsions, moods, and some sort of inner rebellious spirit that can thwart my most generous intentions. I remember seeing a poster one time which said 'There is nothing more powerful than an idea whose time has come.' In other words, there is no scarcity of ideas and good intentions, but, because of our inherent weaknesses, brokenness, and human frailty, there's many a slip twixt the cup and the lip. As the poet said 'The road to hell is paved with good intentions.'

Our sinfulness is a state of being. I speak of a sinful condition. If I went to live at the North Pole I'm still an Irishman. Being a sinner is 'the nature of the beast'. A sinner committing a sin is no great surprise. I am not, I repeat, excusing sin and selfishness. However, I contend that, if I do not accept the reality of my sinful condition, I will flog myself to death with guilt, and that makes a bad situation much worse. In fact, I would go so far as to suggest that holiness involves coming to the conviction that I'm a much greater sinner than I ever thought I was. The story of the Pharisee and the publican contains a central truth about the Christian message. In practice, during my earlier formation, I was put in the Holy of Holies with the Pharisee. I was given all the rules, and I was told that, if I kept those rules to the letter, I would get to heaven. This, of course, was a recipe for disaster, but it took many years of failure, and many discouraging moments to disillusion me about the futility of trying to be good enough to get to heaven. Eventually, I reflected on the story again, and I now believe that I will go to heaven when I die if I can identify with the publican at the back, accept that that is my rightful place, and say from my heart 'Oh God, be merciful to me, a sinner'. Such a person is justified, according to the words of Jesus.

Lord, I often think just how simpler life would be if we only listened to you. You know our human condition, you know what's wrong with us, and you know what will make that right again. Please, Lord, through your Spirit, create within me a genuine desire to be as open as I can to the healing and the reclaiming of salvation and redemption. May your Spirit of truth free me from deceits, denials, and darkness. Amen.

5. Building on weaknesses

When it comes to life, I must surely be confronted with a very definite form of powerlessness. I own nothing. Everything I have is on loan. One heart attack, and it's all over! I was carried into a church, one time, to be baptised, and I wasn't consulted about it, and had no part in that decision. At the end of my life, I will, once again, be carried into a church, and, here again, I will not be involved in that decision. To try to run the show in-between is insanity.

If I try to live my life with any kind of reasonable honesty, I must surely come face to face, again and again, with my own brokenness. I would strongly contend that facing up to this reality is very essential to healthy living. To me, Incarnation is all about God coming to where I'm at, and going much further than that, in that he is willing to go with me, down into the depths of my humanity, my brokenness, and all within me that is in need of redemption, healing, and freedom. Part of the redemption process is to name, claim, and tame my demons. It is very necessary to be in touch with my brokenness. It is a central part of holiness, because God's Spirit works best when human weakness is admitted. God becomes God in my life the moment I stop playing God. It is not possible for a human being to fall on his knees, cry out to God, and not be heard.

It is one of the paradoxes of Christianity that we are most powerful when we are profoundly aware of our weaknesses. The first condition for a miracle is to accept the simple fact that there is nothing I can do. The little woman in the crowd had spent every penny she had over a period of twelve years, all to no avail. NOW she was ready to let Jesus take over. 'If I can only touch the hem of his garment, I will be healed', she said. And, of course, she was. The same with the man who sat by the pool for the previous thirty-eight years. He wasn't getting anywhere, and he now was more than willing to let Jesus take over. I often think of Jesus being on stand-by, waiting for me to admit powerlessness, and then he moves in, and the miracle happens.

God is the supreme and divine composer of the music of the universe, and he conducts the playing of that music. At the beginning of creation, he composed a masterpiece of heavenly harmony. To the thunder clouds, and the ocean he entrusted the percussion section. The wind instruments were the leaves, and the trees. The reeds and the grasses formed the string section, while the birds of the air made up the flutes and pan pipes. The heavy brass instruments were given to the elephants, and other jungle animals, while the special effects were entrusted to the wind, the rivers, and the waterfalls. There was one section of the music that was not scored in any detail, because that was given to humans, and, because they had been created with reason and common sense, it was hoped and expected that they would have enough of what it takes to blend in, and to harmonise with the rest of God's creation. And so, the music began. In every sense, it was heavenly, and out of this world. Day after day was marked by the beauty and balance of God's creation. And then, one day, the unthinkable happened. There was the screech of a discordant note that resounded throughout the whole of God's creation, and every section of the orchestra went totally silent. There was a whisper 'What was that?' Eventually, the explanation came back: That was people. They refused to go along with God's plan any more. They wanted to do things their way, to go their own way, not to be beholding to God anymore. 'What will happen now?' was the worried whisper. 'What will God do now?' The suggestions were many and varied. 'Will he tear up the score, and scrap the whole idea? Perhaps write a whole new piece, and exclude the human dimension?' 'One thing he cannot do' whispered the wind. 'He cannot pretend that nothing happened, because that discordant note will echo and re-echo throughout the universe for all eternity.' And guess what God did? Something, I would suggest that only God would think of. He reached into the midst of every sound that ever was, and he found that one discordant note, and, using that as a theme, he wrote a whole new, and beautiful melody around it. With the mastery that only God can employ, he wove that discordant note into a heavenly melody, of eternal beauty. Each time the discordant note was repeated in the score, it was woven into a whole new vibrancy, that picked it up, as it were, and lifted it to new heights, and gave it a life that it never could reach by itself.

And that is the kind of God we have. A God that takes our weaknesses, our sins, and our brokenness, and turns them into something beautiful, and a joy forever. 'Something beautiful, something good, all my confusion he understood. All I had to offer him was brokenness and strife, but he made something beautiful of my life.'

I would push the point much further, however, by asserting that my very sins can become a path to holiness and salvation. Compassion is a beautiful gift. It literally means to enter into the suffering of others, and to feel their pain, to unscrew the top of their heads, look out through their eyes, and try to see the things they see. Compassion is not something I can learn from a book. Any compassion I have in life has come directly from my own brokenness. The only value the past has are the lessons it taught me. I could be a very wise person today if I learned every lesson life taught me. Twelve Step programmes, such as Alcoholics Anonymous, which are profoundly spiritual, and consistently powerful, are based on the simple premise that no one can effectively help an alcoholic as much as another alcoholic. In other words, because of my own experience of brokenness, and powerlessness, I, alone can understand what you are going through. In a programme, such as A.A., we see a wonderful example of God taking the discordant note of powerlessness in the lives of two men, fifty years ago, and writing a score of extraordinary beauty and power. I am not at all excusing selfishness and sin. What I am saying, however, is that God is quite capable of continuing to write straight on crooked lines. He is quite capable, and always more than willing, to take our brokenness, and turn the whole lot into an eternal good. The whole story of salvation clearly illustrates this. In human terms, the Garden was a disaster, as, indeed, was Calvary. And yet, Augustine, referring to the Fall, says 'Oh happy fault, that merited so great a Redeemer.'

In my own experience of life, I am deeply conscious of the fact that, if God offered me perfection, I would have no hesitation in turning it down! 'There is no one good but God', Jesus told the rich young man. My experience of brokenness and sin is the one thing that qualifies me to care for my fellow struggler. I continue to be open to admitting to every discordant note that sounds within me, and, with total trust in a God of infinite compassion, I look to him to redeem, to rescue, and to heal me.

Heavenly Father, I thank you for the extraordinary rescue-package of salvation and redemption you unveiled in Jesus. Just to think that those things in me that bother and discourage me most, are the very things that you select, through which to show your love and your power! My very weaknesses become the material with which you build the kingdom, because your power is seen best against such a background. Thank you, Lord, and thank you especially for letting me see that, and be part of it. Amen.

6. It's never my fault

Jesus tells us that his Spirit is a Spirit of truth, and that he will lead us into all truth, and the truth will set us free. Denial is something that began back in the Garden. Adam blamed Eve, and Eve blamed the devil, and we're doing that since! The first stage of recovery, from anything, is to admit what is wrong, and what must be set right. Once an alcoholic is prepared to accept the truth about his alcoholism, he has taken the first giant step towards recovery.

It is interesting, and very enlightening, to watch how Jesus handles certain situations in the Gospel. The woman at the well was going on and on about where and how we should worship. Jesus turned to her, and, with tongue in cheek, as it were, he asked her to go home and call her husband! That shut her up very quickly, because she already had nine husbands, and the man she now lived with was not her husband. In other words, stop the waffling! On another occasion, he asked his apostles what they were talking about, as they walked along the road. That rivetted them to the spot, because they had an argument going about which of them was the greatest, something that was, of course, totally against everything he had ever told them about how he saw things. Jesus had the knack of confronting with the truth. 'Do you want to be healed? Who do you say I am? Will you also go away? Do you believe I can heal you?'

Part of the redeeming process is to be willing to confess what is in need of redemption. On the other hand, it is not always that simple. Because of the deviousness of the human mind, I may well be the last person on earth to actually know what's wrong with me. Blaming others for what's wrong with me is fairly common. To confess that I did wrong may not be as mature a stance as at first seems, because I then can go on to blame anybody and everything for causing me to do the wrong. To confess that 'I am wrong' is to accept responsibility for my actions, and to ensure that the buck stops with me. Making my own honest responses, choices, and decisions, enables me grow into becoming more responsible. It is only in this way that I can ever reach peace, freedom, and integrity.

> A certain man went to work every morning at the same time, with the same lunch-box under his arm. At exactly one o'clock each day he entered the shed where the men ate their lunch. The lunch-box was opened, and one of the sandwiches was removed. With the same consistency of every other day, the sandwich was unwrapped, the slices of bread were separated, to be followed by the predictable groan 'Oh no, not cheese again!' This went on day after day, until, finally, some of his work-mates had enough, and one of them turned to him, and asked 'Look, man, why don't you ask your wife to put something else in the sandwiches?' To which the man replied 'What wife? I'm not married.' 'Well, then, who, makes your sandwiches?', to which our hero replied 'I do'.

A very important, beginning, stage in most recovery programmes is to look at my life, as it is, and to be able to say 'I am where I am, and my life is the way it is, because of ME'. (Obviously, this would not apply in the case of victims of abuse, physical or sexual, or the victims of alcoholism in a family). It is important, as I look at my life, that I ask 'Who is making the sandwiches? Who is responsible for my life being the way it is?' I have heard alcoholics blame alcohol for the way their lives are, but I always wait, in the hope, that they will take responsibility for the fact that they are the ones who are drinking the alcohol! It is one of the simplest, and yet most profound statements ever made, that 'the truth will set you free.' This is more a question of facing the truth, rather than allocating blame. It is a fundamental flaw in our psyche, resulting from our damaged condition, to try to blame everybody else for what is wrong with us. Denial is as old as original sin itself.

The first stage of recovery is to break free of denial, and to take responsibility for the way things are. I like the reference to the Prodigal Son 'coming to his senses'. In other words, he opened his eyes, his ears, he got in touch with reality. In a way, he woke up, and saw things as they were. That is, primarily, the work of God's Spirit, who is appropriately called 'The Spirit of Truth'. Jesus speaks of his mission as giving sight to the blind, bringing light to those in darkness, and in the shadow of death. Lies, deceit, and denial are mediums of death. When Adam and Eve fell for the lie in the Garden, they came under new management, as it were. They hid, because they were afraid, and, in many ways, that tendency to hide is still with us. When Jesus came, he was very definite in pointing out where the problem lay. He said that Satan was a liar, and the father of lies. He invited people to come out of darkness, to walk in the light, and not to be afraid.

There was a man one time who picked up the morning paper, and, to his horror, he read his own death notice. The newspapers had reported the death of the wrong man. The caption read 'Dynamite King dies'. The story identified him as a merchant of death. He was the inventor of dynamite, and he had amassed a great fortune through the manufacture of weapons of destruction. Moved by this disturbing experience, he radically changed his whole attitude, and his commitment to life. A healing power, greater than the destructive force of dynamite came over him. It was his moment of Pentecost. From then on, he devoted his full energy and money to works of peace and human betterment. Today he is best remembered as the founder of the Nobel Peace Prize. His name was Alfred Nobel.

> *Lord, I would dearly love to be honest, to be free from self-deceit, and to be as open to truth as is possible. I believe that it is your Spirit who has put that desire within me. I trust, then, that that desire would not be placed in me, without the available grace to act on it. Spirit of Truth, please lead me along the path of truth. Let the scales fall from my eyes each day, until that great day when they will be open wide in wonder, joy, and amazement for all eternity. Amen.*

7. Last and final testament

Prayer is a very personal thing, and I am always ill-at-ease with methods that are very restrictive and structured. Prayer, after all, is really what God does. It is the Spirit in our hearts finding expression through our words or our silences. The Bible can be a powerful source of prayer, but, here again, this need not be too restrictive. If I think of the Gospel as something that is happening now, and I am every person in it, it can help me enter into any particular scene, and be part of it. Once again, I repeat that a life without reflection is a life that is not worth living.

The following story should help to give a whole new meaning to one particular part of the Gospel, a part, I believe to be very important. This comprises the latter part of St John's gospel, from chapter thirteen onwards. It recounts the Last Supper, and the last will and testament of Jesus. Anyhow, let me get on to the story I am using to make a point, and then we can have a short reflection on the story afterwards.

> There was a young doctor, who was married, with three young children. He had great hopes for them, and he was fully prepared to give them as much of his time and attention as he could, as they grew up. He would be there for them, as they went to school, and as they worked on school projects at home. He would be there when they ran out on the field of sport, or came out on the stage in school performances. Especially, he would be there as they moved into adolescence, to advise and counsel. To him, his role was very much on-going, and he had a great sense of excitement at the prospects for the future.

Which was all very well, until about his thirtieth birthday, when he discovered he had cancer, and he had little time left to do all the things he had dreamed of. He was devastated. His whole world came tumbling down around his ears. For a few days, he didn't know what to do, and which way to turn. Eventually, he came up with an idea that might help salvage some of his dreams. He got a tape-recorder, and a few c-90 tapes, and he proceeded to pour out his heart to his children. He knew that, right now, they were too young to understand anything of what was happening, or anything he wanted to say to them. These tapes, however, were an investment in the future.

He told them how much he loved them, and how, even if he now has to go on to the third and final stage of his own journey in life, he would continue to pray for them, and to watch out for them. He told them all he had learned about life, about the mistakes he had made, how he had learned from those mistakes, and how they might best be able to avoid many of the pit-falls that lurk along the journey of life. He asked them to look out for each other, and how they could honour his memory, and make him proud of them, by the way in which they grew up to be become mature, responsible citizens.

Looking at life, from his present perspective, he told them what he now considers to be the most important priorities in life, and how they could avoid those things that destroy, and nurture those things which give life. He bared his soul to them, in a way that no father has ever spoken to his children. He accepted the fact that it might well be years from now before they could fully understand what he was sharing with them, and he counselled them to be gentle and patient with themselves, until life, itself, had helped them arrive at the necessary level of maturity, to be able to absorb all that he now shared with them.

Those tapes were a profound legacy of wisdom. There was not a surplus word, and no one could possibly question the total sincerity of the speaker. There was a depth of wisdom, and a sense of urgency in all he shared with them. He knew well that it would be years later before the full import of what he had to say would mean anything to them. He was deeply aware that he was speaking from the unique perspective of someone who has reached the end of the journey, and, therefore, he did not expect that his vision should be shared by someone who is only starting out on the journey.

The father died, and, as time went by, the mother began to intro-
duce her children to whatever parts of the tapes she thought they
could understand. It was a very gradual process, and some part of
the tapes began to play an ever-increasing part in special occasions,
like his anniversary, or a child's birthday. As each child reached a
certain age, the mother made copies of the tapes, so that, eventually,
each had a personal collection. Throughout the following years,
those tapes took on a life of their own. They were a veritable blue-
print for life. The father spoke openly and honestly about adoles-
cence, about the pit-falls of college-life, and about the criteria one
should apply to relationships, to religion, and to the many and varied options the world offers us on the journey of life. In a way, it
was like a map, to guide the traveller through an area that was
somewhat of a mine-field.

Those tapes were a source of wisdom and direction. They were carried forth into the next generation, and became something of a family heirloom. In a most extraordinary way, they became so much
more than the man who recorded them could ever have expected.
In fact, one would be tempted to surmise if they were not a greater
influence for life and living, than if the father himself had lived to
speak those words. By way of general summation, it is accepted
that those tapes succeeded beyond the wildest dreams of the man
who recorded them.

And that brings me back to what I was speaking about, before I told
the story. In John's gospel, from chapter thirteen onwards, we have
several c-90s from Jesus, just before he died. He told his apostles
that he knew they were sad because he was about to leave them, but
it was for their good that he was going. If he did not go, the Holy
Spirit would not come; but, if he went, he would send the Spirit,
and then they would have the same Spirit and power that he had.

He told them how much he loved them, and he prayed that they
would know that the Father loved them as much as He loved Jesus.
He promised that he would never abandon them, or leave them in
the storm. He would send them the Holy Spirit, who would be with
them always, remind them of everything he had told them, and
lead them into all truth.

He told them that he depended on them for several things. Firstly, people would know they belonged to him by the evidence of their love for each other. Secondly, it is through the evidence of their being of one mind and heart that the world would believe the Father had sent him. He was very specific, and most detailed about how they were to love one another. He had knelt at their feet with a basin of water and a towel, like any slave of his day, and he washed their feet. He then told them that this was greatness in his scale of things, i.e., through the power of humble service. He gave them a new commandment, telling them to love one another as he loved them.

He promised to prepare a place for them, and, when the time was ripe, he would come and bring them, so that, where he was, they also might be. He told them not to be worried or afraid, because he had overcome their enemies, and they now could share in his victory.

And that, my friends, is the last will and testament of Jesus. It is a rich source for reflection, and for prayer. It gives extraordinary insights into the mind of Jesus, and will greatly enrich those who take time out to dwell on it. As with the young doctor, and his family, who ended up with the contents of his message almost entirely committed to memory, we are offered this wonderful treasure of inspiration, encouragement, and reassurance. May we fully accept the gift that it is, and benefit fully from the very special riches it contains.

> *Thank you, Jesus for the message you left us as a final will and testament. Thank you for the many promises, and all the love it contains. With all my heart, I pray that your Spirit might lead me more and more into accepting and owning that message. I can play that tape any day I want to, and be sure that the words are meant for me right here, right now. Thank you, Lord. Amen.*

8. Unconditional love

We are human, and, by ourselves, we can live only within the limits that such a condition imposes. It is not part of our nature to love unconditionally. Despite all our best efforts, there are layers and layers of selfishness within us, and the human heart can be a veritable mine-field of preferences, prejudices, and preconceived ideas. Part of being human is that we work on some sort of short fuse, that leaves us subject to mood swings, and to feelings of insecurity about our own possessions, investments, and interests, whether these be emotional, or physical. The word 'human' comes from the Latin, *humus*, meaning clay. There is no way that, by myself, I can raise myself above my human condition. Part of being human is to be mortal. I will die, and so will anything I do, of myself. By myself, I can do good, but it cannot last. It is like a tape-recorder, with batteries, which will play, of course, but which just cannot continue to play for any length of time.

Only God can love without conditions, and without limits. Only God can love with a love that will continue, and is not deflected by anything the other person does. God loves me exactly as I am. Whether I'm good or bad makes no difference. God loves me because he is good, totally independently of what kind of person I am.

Sometimes we come across a parent or a spouse who, through their love for another, gives us some glimpse into the way God loves us. He seems to be able to love no matter what the other person does. This is extraordinary, and very unusual. I always contend that it is through people that I grow in my insights into God. I have witnessed Gospel values being lived, and being really effective in the lives of individuals, and this has helped enormously in the growth of my own faith.

Some time ago, I met a missionary home on holidays from Kenya. He had spent the previous thirty years there, and it was obvious he had developed an extraordinary love and respect for the peoples of that country. He was very conscious of how, in many ways, they had a richness of spirit, and of tradition, not often encountered in our Western world. I was fascinated by his accounts of various experiences he had there, and how he himself had been greatly enriched through his years spent among the people. He was a wonderful story-teller, and I share one of his stories here, because I myself was deeply touched when I first heard it.

On the first Saturday of every month, he drove his jeep out into the bush, to round up those who needed the services of the flying doctors, who came to his clinic once a month. Each month, the doctors tried to concentrate on some particular kind of ailment. On this particular Saturday, he collected those with hair-lips, and cleft palates. As was usual, especially when a child was involved, several family members came along as well. As the morning progressed, those whose surgery was completed, began to emerge from the clinic. The priest was particularly struck by a young boy coming out of the clinic. He had a hair-lip, and the transformation effected by the surgeon was nothing short of miraculous. It was a really beautiful job, and, except for close examination, there was no evidence of the malformation that had been there all his life. The priest brought the young lad over to his father, who was seated under a tree. The boy bowed to his father, and, as is the custom, the father placed his hand on the boy's head by way of blessing. That was it! Not a word passed between them, and the father did not seem to notice the transformation in the boy's appearance.

The priest then brought the boy over to his mother, and to other members of his family, and here, the reception was totally different. They went wild with excitement. The boy was brought out into the full light, his upper lip was examined in great detail, and he was hugged by all his family, amidst tears, and cries of gladness. Meanwhile, the father remained seated under the tree. This puzzled, and slightly annoyed the priest. He approached the father and asked 'Are you pleased with the job the doctor

did on your son?', to which the father replied 'Oh, I am indeed."
'Well', said the priest 'you certainly didn't show any great sign
of being pleased, when I brought him out to you a short while
ago.' The father looked at the priest, and replied with sincerity,
and quiet conviction 'I love my son. If I showed any great excitement when I saw the vast improvement in his appearance, that
might cause him to think that I hadn't really loved him when he
had a hair-lip. I don't love him any more now than I loved him
before he had the surgery.'

I pass this story on, now, because I believe it gives a very clear and
simple insight into the way God loves us. God loves us, because
that's what God does best. He could not possibly love us 50%, or
even 99%. God loves us, and accepts us exactly as we are, at any one
time. I could understand how a purely religious person could well
be troubled by this story. Religion, which can be based on what we
do, can create the myth that salvation is something that must be
earned. That is not true. Salvation is something that has to be
accepted. God gives me nothing, while offering me everything.
Faith is a response to love. The greatest thanks I can offer Jesus for
what he has done for me is to accept with gratitude all that he died
to earn for me. Humility is another word for truth, and the truth is
that I just do not have what it takes to earn or merit my own salvation. God believes that, and that is why Jesus came, to do for us
something that we never could do for ourselves. Jesus said 'No one
knows the Father except the Son, and those to whom the Son chooses to reveal Him.' It is a very special grace to know the love of the
Father. His love is there for us, whether we have hair-lips or not.

There's a story of a grandmother, a mother, and a little boy, three
generations, who went into a restaurant, and sat down to order. The
waitress took the grandmother's order, the mother's order, and
then turned to the little boy, and said 'What would you like?' The
mother immediately said 'Oh, I'll order for him.' The waitress,
without being overly rude, ignored the mother, and again said to
the little boy 'What would you like?' Glancing over at his mother, to
see how she was reacting to this, the little boy said 'Eh, eh, I'd like a
hamburger'. 'How would you like your hamburger? With mustard
and pickles and the works?' asked the waitress. With his mouth
dropping open in amazement now, he said 'The works, the works.'

The waitress went over to the hatch, and she called out the grand-mother's order and the mother's order. Then in a very loud voice she said 'And a hamburger with the works'. The little boy turned to his mother in utter astonishment and said 'Mammy, mammy, she thinks I'm real'!

I have added this extra story as part of the reflection, because in God's eyes you are very very real, and he really does care about what is wrong with you, what your needs are, and what you say when you speak. He loves you, just as you are, and he loves every-thing about you.

Heavenly Father, unless your Spirit leads me into the secrets of the kingdom, I could never hope to grasp the extent of your unconditional love. I have to trust that it must be your will that I continue to grow into a deeper conviction of the reality of that love. I certainly want to know it, and to be deeply conscious of it. I open my heart to it, and trust your Spirit to do the rest. Thank you. Amen.

9. Some important words

I continue the theme of the Father's love in yet another story. In travelling anywhere in life, I have to begin from where I'm at. Life is constantly bringing us from the known to the unknown. Grace builds on nature, rather than replacing it. There is not much point in speaking to someone about God as a loving Father, if that person never actually experienced a father's love. I was reminded of that, one time, as I spoke with a girl whose father was in gaol for murdering her mother. On the other hand, through my better experiences of human love and relationships, I can get a very healthy appreciation of a God who is Father, and who loves each of us as his children.

Susan was eleven years of age, and she had some rare form of cancer. The general hospital in her part of the country was unable to meet the pain level at which she suffered, and, so, she was transferred to a hospice situation, where the proper levels of pain-killers were more readily available. There was a family conference in her home, and it was decided that her dad should accompany her during this time away from home. He travelled to Dublin with her, and found suitable accommodation close-by. By breakfast-time each morning, he was with her in the ward, and he spent the whole day there, until she went to sleep at night. When she was strong enough, he brought her for walks around the grounds. On occasions, he brought her to some of the local shops. She saw a budgie on one of the floors in the hospice, and was so much excited about it, that her father went out, and arrived back with a budgie and cage just for her. Every Thursday, they were joined by her mother, brothers and sisters, who were driven to Dublin by a family friend.

As the weeks went by, there was a marked deterioration in Susan's condition. At times her dad was seen to be helping her faltering steps along a corridor, or pushing her in a wheelchair around the grounds. Eventually, he was to be seen sitting by her bed, holding her hand. Susan was a smart kid, and, over many weeks there, she had seen several of those around her being wheeled, in their beds, very discreetly, into an adjoining room, and they did not return. She asked her dad if she, too, was going to die? She had many such questions over those weeks, and her dad discovered a strength that he never dreamed he had. He was with her, as were all the rest of her family, as she died.

I titled this story 'Some Important Words', and now I hope to explain that, as well as share the very clear lessons that were so evident throughout those weeks in the hospice. Susan knew that her dad loved her. She didn't need me, or anyone else to tell her that. She could see this for herself, day after day. And that, for me, was an image of what God had in mind, in the Garden, at the beginning of Creation. People would see for themselves how he was caring and providing for them, and he didn't need preachers or teachers to convince anyone of that fact.

(At this stage, I must digress, while, hopefully, not losing the threads of the story. God does not change. He is the same yesterday, today, and always. At the time of the Fall, it was people who walked away, as it were. Jesus came to invite us back to the Garden, and, even if we got pigs food all over our faces, he assures us that there is a big hug awaiting us. In this way, I believe the Garden is still on offer, and God's love can be as tangible and as evident in our lives as her father's love was to Susan.)

Because Susan knew her father loved her, she trusted him completely. Faith and trust is a response to love. Please don't ask me to trust someone until you convince me that this person is genuinely interested in my welfare. Susan felt O.K. about leaving home, and coming to a hospital in Dublin, once she knew that her dad was coming with her. No point in telling people to trust God until they are helped to come to the conclusion that he really does love them, and holds their welfare very dear to his heart.

Because Susan trusted her father, she obeyed him in everything. She knew he would not ask her to do something that was not for her good, and so she felt sufficient confidence to be led by what he told her. If he thought she should rest, she did so. If he suggested she should come for a walk, she immediately got ready to do so. For her, it wasn't really a question of obedience, as much as co-operating with what her dad saw to be best for her. Jesus said 'If you love me, you will obey me...'. In other words, if you trust me, and have faith in me, you will do what I ask of you, because you are the ones who will benefit, as a result.

Lastly, because Susan trusted her dad, she was not afraid. She knew that he would be there for her, come what may. As I said earlier, she asked him if she, too, was going to die, and he was able to talk to her about that, without generating any great level of anxiety, or fear. Again and again, in the Gospels, Jesus tells us not to be afraid. He wanted us to know that we had nothing to fear, because he would never abandon us, or leave us in the storm.

I suggested, in a previous paragraph, that the Garden was still on offer. I should not wait till I die to return there. The invitation is issued, and the Father is anxiously awaiting our return, to come back to the fullness of his love and acceptance. There is a legend about the Day of Judgement. The gates of heaven are open, and God's family is entering in, filled with songs of joy, praise, and thanksgiving. Jesus is seen standing at the gates, looking off into the distance. When asked why he was doing so, he said that he was waiting for Judas.

> *Heavenly Father, your love is the highest form of the most unselfish fatherly love this world could ever know. Jesus came to show us that love. He spoke of you with joy and excitement, because he experienced and knew your love on a moment-to-moment basis. He spoke of something that was central to his mission. I ask you, Jesus, please reveal your Father's love to me. Please let me come to see even a glimpse of what you saw clearly. Amen.*

10. Are you looking for Jesus?

One of the great chants of high-powered evangelists has to do with 'finding the Lord'. 'Have you found the Lord?'. There was a man in my home town, when I was a kid, and he was accepted to be simple, if harmless. He gate-crashed every gathering in church, chapel, or orange hall. One day, down in the market square, a preacher-man was holding forth about finding the Lord, when he spotted our hero in the front row, in what appeared to be some sort of trance. (For those who knew him, it was his usual vacant stare!) Anyhow, the preacher stopped, and turned to him with the question 'My dear man, have you found the Lord?', to which our hero replied 'Naw, did you lose him?' For once the man was brilliant, and the question was stupid.

It is not the Lord who is lost! Incarnation is about God coming to where I'm at. Jesus speak of leaving ninety-nine sheep, to go after one that is lost. He speaks of searching till the sheep is found. He speaks of a woman searching for a lost coin, until she finds it. He said that he came to seek and to find those who are lost, thus confirming the prophecy of the father of John the Baptist, who said that the Lord would visit his people, to bring light to those in darkness, and in the shadow of death, and to guide their feet into the way of peace.

Finding the Lord contains the germ of a deep-rooted human disease, which insists on turning the divine initiative into human endeavour. Religion tends to be about control, while spirituality is about surrender. Religion is more about what we do for God, and spirituality is about what God does for, in, and through us, when we let him. Spirituality would have us trust God to come to us, even if we were on Skid Row. I am not implying that there is anything automatic about this, because there is not. God coming to me is in

response to my cry for help, or my acceptance of my powerlessness.
It is not possible for me to fall on my knees, cry out to God, and not
be heard.

I share the following story with tongue in cheek, while being serious about the simple message it contains.

> The telephone rang in a house, and was answered by a tiny
> whispered voice 'Hello'. 'Can I speak to your father?' asked the
> caller. 'No, I'm sorry, he's busy', came the whispered reply.
> 'Well, can I speak to your mother?' And, once again, the whisper
> 'No, I'm sorry, she's busy.' The caller tried a different angle. 'Is
> there anyone else there?' 'Yes', came the one-word whispered
> response. The caller was beginning to get annoyed, but he strug-
> gled to keep his cool, as he asked 'Who else is there?' 'There's the
> fire brigade, the police, and an ambulance' the little voice whis-
> pered, without any great emotion or feeling. 'Can I speak to one
> of the men from the fire brigade?' asked the caller, to whom he
> received the, by now, almost predictable whispered reply 'No,
> I'm sorry, they're busy.' 'Well, can I speak to the driver of the
> ambulance?' asked the caller, by now running rapidly out of
> patience. 'No, I'm sorry, he's busy' came back the whisper. The
> caller raised his voice, determined to assert his authority, and to
> take control of the situation. 'Tell one of the police that I want to
> speak to him now', he shouted. And, once again, to his total
> frustration, came the calm and whispered reply 'No, I'm sorry,
> they're busy.' This brought one final outburst from the caller
> 'What's happening there? What are they all doing there?', and
> back came the final whispered reply 'They're looking for me'!!

I said, before sharing this story, that I did so with tongue in cheek,
because I think it is both funny, and very appropriate to teach
something I consider to be important. I think of Jesus as the young
lad in the story, and he's watching all those people out there, in a
total frenzy, searching for him. Someone said one time that, if God
wanted to really hide on us, he would come to live in our hearts,
because it is reckoned that few people would ever think of looking
for him there! Christianity is about what happens in the heart. It is a
long journey from the head to the heart. Living in the head is one
way of describing living with the values of the world, where everything and everyone is subjected to the microscope of my intelli-

gence, and is judged in terms of usefulness, and importance, by worldly standards. According to Jesus, every one of us is on this earth with as much right as anyone else. The most handicapped person is on this earth with as much right as the greatest genius that ever lived. God is the creator, who acts out of love at all times. It is only when I begin to see others with the vision of God that I can ever have any hope of appreciating the uniqueness of each individual. I believe that Jesus is just as present in a wheelchair in a nursing home than he is in the tabernacle down in the chapel. God can be present in as many ways as he chooses to be, and, until we accept that simple fact, we will pass him by, without noticing him, a thousand times a day.

In the gospels, the apostles finally catch up with Jesus, who had slipped away after the miracle of the loaves and fishes, and they told him 'Everyone is looking for you.' The words of the Psalmist would merit reflection here 'Seek the Lord where he may be found.' In the letter to the Hebrews, we read 'No one draws near to God without first believing that he exists, and that he rewards those who seek him.' Jesus says that he came to 'seek and to find the lost among the children of Israel'. If I am prepared to be found by him, he certainly will come to where I'm at. God is totally a God of now, and if I can become a person of now, I will certainly meet him. The problem often is that part of me can be back in the past, called regret or guilt, while the rest of me can be in the future, called worry, and there may be very little of me present in the now. I could well imagine that many people meet God for the first time at the moment of death, when the hiding, the evading, and the running is over, and there is no place left to hide.

If I may throw in another short story here on the subject of seeking the Lord. A young lad went up to an old monk, one time, and told him he was looking for God, and he wanted to know where or how he might find him. The monk brought the lad down to a river, put him in the water, and held his head under the water, until he nearly drowned. When he lifted the lad's head out of the water, there was a loud gasp, as the boy filled his lungs with much-wanted air. Then the monk told him 'When you want God as much as you wanted that breath of air, you'll certainly find him!'

Thank you, Jesus, for your patience! You have told us clearly where you are to be found. You are found wherever people are broken, suffering, or marginalised. You are present in us, even when we're not at all happy with who we are or how we are. You are always waiting for us to turn to you. Without you, we are lost. Amen

11. Rescued and redeemed

In contrast to that last story about finding the Lord, I now include one about the Lord finding us. I cannot stress enough the central theme of Incarnation, where God comes down to join us on the journey, and to share the burdens of life with us. He could have loved us from a distance, but he decided not to. For God, love was clearly a decision. He had created us, and when we got it completely wrong, he would recreate us.

He would seek us, and find us, and then, like Moses with the Israelites, he would lead us safely all the way home. Sometimes we hear it said that someone is very scattered, someone else is all over the place, and yet another badly needs to get herself together! The opposite to that is wholeness, togetherness, or simply holiness. God is holy, and I am venturing the idea that each of us is part of who God is, and it is his biggest priority that not one of us should remain alienated from him. However, because of free-will, God cannot compel us to belong to him. In the story of the Prodigal Son, the father waited for the son to return, and had a big hug waiting for him, when he did so. He would not, however, go to where the son was feeding the pigs, take him by the ear, and frog-march him home! No way. The son had to 'come to his senses', look at his situation, as it was, and make his own decision. The highlight of the story is not the hug at the point of home-coming, but the moment of grace when the son's senses were turned on. He opened his eyes, his ears, and his hands, and the full horror of his situation hit him. Then, and only then, was he ready to move. There is nothing more powerful than an idea whose time has come!

There was a young lad who grew up by the sea. He had a deep love for boats, and all his spare time was spent around boats of one kind or another. One day, he picked up a bit of a log, and, to while away an idle hour, he began to carve it. He was working away without any particular pattern in his head, when, suddenly, he got the idea of carving a boat. This really excited him, because he had a very clear idea in his mind how a boat should be shaped. He slowed down in his task, because this was a labour of love, and he wanted to give it his whole and undivided attention.

He worked away during every spare moment, and, with his inner image of his ideal boat, he saw that his project was coming along very well indeed. This was not going to be some plain or ordinary boat. He finished the carving, and there was still much to do. It had to be polished, and painted, which he did with his own favourite colours. He cut everything in exact proportion, and he rigged it out with sails, rigging, and rudder. He finally put a name on it, which he very deliberately chose, and painted on the side.

The job was done, and he was really proud of his handiwork. It drew much admiration and attention from those who saw it. For him, there was one important, final, step to go. Boats belonged in water, and, so, he just had to bring it down to the harbour, for his own private ceremony of launching. He put it in the water, and he watched, with swelling pride, as it bobbed up and down on the little waves. Its colours looked really attractive, and how he wished that everyone was here, to see what he could see.

Something began to happen, that was so gradual, the boy himself was totally unaware of it at first. The breeze filled the tiny sails, and, bit by bit, the boat began to drift away from him. He was so rapt in admiration, that it took some time to realise that the boat was, actually, drifting out beyond his reach. Instinctively, he called it, as if it knew its name, and would respond to his call. This boat was so much part of him that he forgot, by providing sails, he had actually given it a will of its own. To his deep shock and horror, he stood there helpless, as he watched his master-piece drift away out to sea. There was no one there to help him, and he experienced total powerlessness. He had no choice but to turn around, and walk back home, completely bereft of the excitement and joy he experienced, when he had come down to the water.

He slept very little that night. His every waking moment was filled with thoughts about the boat. His heart was heavy, and his attention in school was limited, because, in a way, he carried the boat with him, in his heart. It was some weeks later, and he was window-shopping down town. He was staring aimlessly into a shop window, when, like a bolt of lightening, he was fully alert. There, in the window, amidst all the toys, was his boat! He rushed in, and asked for it, and he was so excited that his attempts to explain to the shop-keeper what had happened, all came out wrong. Anyhow, the shop-keeper was having none of it, and the boy was told that, if he wanted the boat, he would just have to buy it, as with every other toy in the shop. 'The boat is mine now', said the shop-keeper, 'and it only becomes yours if you pay for it.'

The boy rushed home, all flustered and excited, and told his father the situation regarding the boat. The father explained that, yes, he would have to buy the boat, if he wanted to get it back. 'How much will I have to pay for it?' asked the boy. 'That depends', said the father. 'If you really want it, you will give everything you have to buy it.' The boy emptied every saving box and piggy bank he had, and, without counting the money, he put the lot in a box, and ran all the way back to the shop. He popped the box on the counter, and, again, without counting it, the shop-keeper took the money, and handed the boat to the boy.

The boy ran out the door, and once out in broad daylight, he rubbed the boat, kissed it, and began to polish it with his sleeve. He ran all the way back home, where he met his father. 'So the boat is yours now?' asked the father. 'Yes, dad, it's mine now', said the boy excitedly, 'except that this time it's mine twice over. I made it, and now I have bought it back, and I have given every-thing I have to get it. Yes, indeed, it certainly is mine now!'

The word 'redeem' comes from the language used in times of slav-ery. If I had money, and had a compassionate nature, I could buy a slave from someone, and then give that slave his liberty, and he was no longer a slave. I redeemed him, and he was now free. We some-times hear the same word used in connection with pawn shops. Someone may be badly stuck for ready cash, and is forced to take some household item, or family possession, down to the local pawn shop, and exchange it for money. A few days later, if the money is available, that person may be very anxious to return to the pawn shop to redeem that item from the control and possession of another, and to return it where it belongs.

We say 'Lord, by your cross and resurrection, you have set us free. You are the redeemer of the world.' It may not be easy to grasp the full implications of that statement, because, as Jesus told Peter, flesh and blood cannot reveal such things. This is especially the work of the Spirit, who, according to Jesus, will teach us all things, remind us of everything he told us, and bring us into all truth. To know Jesus as my personal Saviour and Redeemer, to accept him as such, to let him redeem and save me, and, finally, to experience redemption and salvation in my life, ... that is the answer to the question 'Are you saved?' To know that I am saved brings the extra responsibility of the witness value of such, when I begin to look saved!!

It is important that I reflect on the implications resulting from the words this story has put into the mouth of Jesus. 'We belong to him. He made us, and, when we were in slavery, because of original sin, he bought us back, redeemed us, and, in the process, he gave everything he had to do so.' As Jesus himself put it 'Greater love than this no one has, than that a person should lay down his life for a friend.'

Holy Spirit, Spirit and Breath of God! The love of God shown in salvation and redemption is something that my little mind could never hope to comprehend. Please know, however, that I really don't wish that my mind could understand it. All I ask is that my heart may be open to it, and that my spirit might experience it. This is something that is beyond me, and I depend on you totally for this one. Amen.

12. If I have not love

On my own journey in life, I can clearly identify a very definite awakening to the basic and central truth that God loved me, and how much that should, and could influence and effect my whole attitude towards God. Naturally, I had often heard reference to God's love, but, somehow, it seemed to be a love that was laced with justice, that had many conditions attaching, and was very difficult to merit.

The idea that GOD IS LOVE, and the full implications of that, were entirely lost on me. It was a moment of revelation for me when I understood renewal in the Church as something like this: Jesus died to bring people across a bridge from a love of law into a law of love. Two thousand years later, the church had gone back over that bridge again, into a love of law. Pope John XXIII, bless him, went on his knees, and asked God for another Pentecost (thereby, implying that we blew that last one!) He got a new Pentecost, and we are now living in the Acts of the Apostles of that Second Pentecost. It's a long and tough haul back: back from religion into spirituality, from human endeavour into pure gift of God, from law to love.

It is important that this be approached with gentleness, compassion, and understanding. In practice, what's involved is that good people, very good people, were told what to do, and they did that with total commitment for many years, and passed that on to succeeding generations. NOW they have to be told that, through no fault of their own, they have lost sight of some of the most important and central messages in the Gospels. Some time ago I wrote an article which referred to about twenty 'sins' of my youth, which, we now accept as not being sins at all! (Eating meat on Fridays, fasting from midnight, etc., etc., as well as two 'reserved' sins in my own diocese from that time, i.e., making poteen (illegal liquor), and going to dances during Lent!)

The 'old' approach, if I may call it that, was based largely on externals. Going to Mass, novenas, and parish missions may have had more to do with the social life of those times, than with spiritual encounters with God, that would lead to wholeness, healing, and holiness. It is not uncommon to encounter a veritable Third World, in terms of spiritual maturity, right here among our church-going public. I heard of a man, over eighty years of age, who still confessed to not doing what his parents told him, even though they were dead for the past fifty years! This had been part of the list given at the time of his First Confession, and he had never updated that list! I had an uncle who said a prayer every night against having a toothache, and he hadn't a tooth of his own for years! It was part of the night prayers given him by his mother, and it was turned out nightly up to the time of his death!

There was a priest who was about to retire, and he decided he would build himself a bungalow, over-looking the sea. He was a veritable Jack-of-all-trades, and he was quite capable of doing most of the work himself. He was genuinely excited about the prospect, and the idea of, eventually, retiring there with his books, was a dream he had often contemplated.

A year or two before he was due to retire, he began the project. It would, of necessity, be slow, and drawn-out, because it was more of a hobby for the day off, than a full-time occupation. He was happy enough, however, with progress, and soon his dream-house began to take shape. He was pottering away in his spare time, and he availed of professional help only when absolutely necessary. Eventually, he got to the stage where he was hanging the doors, and this was really proving too much for him. He knew there was a special knack in this, and now he was discovering that he didn't have what it takes. He struggled on, with quiet determination, until, one day, the task got too much for him, and he put on his coat, and went for a walk, to work out his frustrations. He must have walked for miles, and, eventually, he found himself in front of a new house nearing completion, and, as luck would have it, there was a carpenter in the process of hanging the front door.

The priest drew nearer to have a look, something which made the carpenter very uneasy, feeling he was being watched. 'Can I help you?' he asked the priest, which was a polite way of asking him if he wanted something! The priest decided to come clean, so he told the carpenter about the problem he was having with the doors of his new bungalow. He asked for advice, and what the carpenter thought were the finer points to watch for in such an operation. The carpenter, who was somewhat of a roguish disposition, looked straight at the priest, and put forward a suggestion. 'Father', he said, 'I'll make a bargain with you. I'll hang all those doors for you, if you'll promise to do something for me.' The priest was immediately on his guard. There just had to be a catch here somewhere! Anyhow, the prospect of having all his doors properly hung was very appealing, so the priest said 'O.K., I agree, but what do you want from me?' 'I have been a member of your church for many years, and Sunday after Sunday I had to sit there listening to you preaching. I couldn't interrupt you. I had no choice but to listen. Now, I'll hang all those doors for you, if you'll let me preach a sermon to you. I must insist, however, that, no matter how much you feel like speaking, you must not interrupt me.' It was a strange request, but the priest readily agreed to it, thinking of the benefits accruing to him, as a result.

The carpenter put the priest in his car, and off they went up the road. The car was stopped some miles away, and they both got out. The priest was brought into a field, and over to what appeared to be the foundation for a house. The outline stakes were down, the foundation had been dug out, and filled with stones and rubble. The concrete had actually been poured for the floors, and it was obvious what the plan for the ground-floor was. However, for some reason, the building had been abandoned, and the foundation was now almost totally covered with nettles, grass, and weeds. The priest looked at the carpenter, but was unable to ask a question, as the carpenter turned back towards the car with the words 'Think about it'.

They drove on for another few miles, and stopped in front of a real show-piece of a house. This was something that would surely catch the eye of the passer-by. It was magnificent. Everything was just perfect. The tiles, the door, windows, drapes, all were of the highest quality. Add to that the neatly manicured lawns, the trimmed bushes, and the tastefully laid-out entrance, and you have a house that would merit ten out of ten in any competition. The carpenter brought the priest up to the front door, opened the door, and ushered him inside. When the priest entered the house, he gave an audible gasp of amazement. The inside of the house was totally vacant; it was a total shell. No ceilings, no dividing walls, no floors, nothing that one expects to be part of the inside of any house. The priest was really puzzled, but, of course, he couldn't say anything, as the carpenter said 'Think about it'.

And then, of course, like the Three Bears, there are three houses! After a mile or two, the car was stopped, and out they got. Once again, they were in front of another house. Not anything as eye-catching as that last house, it still wasn't bad. There was a loose tile on the roof, the drapes on one of the windows were crooked, the gates could do with painting, and the grass was due a mow-ing. They approached the door, which the carpenter opened, announcing 'I'm home, gang'. Immediately he was surrounded by three little kids who swung out of him with sheer delight at seeing him, as they tried the pockets of his overcoat for the sweets which, they knew, were always to be found there. Just then a young woman came out of the kitchen, with a welcoming smile, and she kissed him, and asked him how was his day. Meanwhile, the priest stood there, not sure what to do. He had noticed that a picture on the wall wasn't straight, and there was a school blazer lying on the steps of the stairs. He was snapped out of his reverie by the carpenter, who said 'Oh, sorry ... think about it'.

The following Sunday, as the carpenter sat in the benches in church, he was grinning from ear to ear as he heard the priest speak of the different ways people deal with the Gospel of Jesus Christ. Some, early in life, lay a solid foundation, through the Communion and Confirmation programmes, but they do noth-ing about it after that, and, so, they continue to live with a very childish level of spirituality. (Please make a very clear distinc-tion between childishness and child-likeness!) A second group take the message of the Gospel, and concentrate on doing a mag-nificent external job on it. They are present at everything, and are always seen to be proper and correct in all they do, while, inside, they are empty shells, with no real life there. And then, thank God, there are those who need a lick of paint, a straightening out, a tidying up, from time to time, … but, to those who know them, and see them in action, there is a great deal of love there.

This story is more than just a fanciful parable! I'm sure each of us can identify with each of the houses concerned, and how accurately each of them reflects how things can be with any one of us. St Paul says that, no matter what gifts I have, if I have not love, I have nothing. Christianity is about what happens inside, otherwise, to quote St Paul again, I'm nothing more than sounding brass or clanging cymbal. (I would suggest, in the context of reflecting on this story, that chapter 13 of St Paul's Second letter to the Corinthians would prove to be a real gold-mine).

At the risk of over-labouring this point, I see the first two houses as representing religion, deprived of the soul, the life, the inner vibrancy that comes from spirituality. Jesus, who is meek and humble of heart, has many scathing comments to make about the Pharisees, who laid great emphasis on externals. He said they were like white marble tomb-stones, beautiful to behold, on the outside, but, inside they were full of rotten bones. They cleaned the outside of the cup, while, inside, the cup could be really dirty.

I don't think it takes any profound or prolonged reflection to see the situation where there is only a foundation with no building, or a building with nothing inside. The third situation, as represented by the third house, might merit a little further reflection. I am not talking about perfection here, nor am I advocating perfection. Far from it! There is no such thing as a perfect family. The highest we can hope to achieve is a good-enough family; a family in which the common courtesies operate, and where love is the binding force holding members together. Love is not always plain sailing. If there is enough forgiveness, love will survive. Love is about unity, not uniformity. It is not about producing some sort of Hitler Youth, where all members goose-step together! It is about respecting the individuals, and accepting the differences that make us all individual.

It is generally accepted that St John's gospel is a highly theological presentation, full of imagery. Light and darkness, life and death, flesh and spirit are contrasted. It begins with a poetical flourish, and there is obviously the clear agenda of emphasising that, yes, Jesus is the Son of God. Many years later, when an old man on the Island of Patmos, St John wrote his two letters. These are just a joy to read. They are simple, and they possess, as it were, the result of long reflection on the message of the Master. In summary, they say that we should love one another because God loves us. He places God's love for us above our love for him, and he tells us that it is how we love others that shows whether God lives in us or not. John has reduced the message to the one word LOVE.

> *Lord Jesus, you took on our human nature so that you could be with us, like us, and for us. This was your way of being down-to-earth, of translating love into hugs, tears, wine, and bread. I pray, Lord, for the grace to accept the fact that you want to be down-to-earth with your love, and you want us to begin with what we have. Any growth in our lives happens when your Spirit takes over. Spirit of God, here I am, not much, but it's all I have. You see what's needed ... Thank you. Amen.*

13. A heart transplant

When I speak of being a Christian, it is important to remember that this is something effected in me, by the Spirit of God, and not something I myself can do. It is about Incarnation taking place in me, where my heart becomes a Bethlehem, a Calvary, a Pentecost place. As you read this, it must be patently obvious that this is not something you or I can bring about. It is God alone who creates, and it is God alone who recreates. 'I make all things new' says the Lord. St Paul, with great honesty, speaks of what he experiences within himself. He identifies it as some sort of basic rebelliousness, that keeps opposing all his attempts to do the good. He is conscious of a conflict going within, between the forces of good and evil, which he identifies as his old nature, and his new nature. The old nature is me, before Incarnation takes place, and the new nature is that power that comes from the Spirit living within. The problem is, of course, that the old nature doesn't disappear! I will always be a sinner. Now, however, through what Jesus has made possible, I can have access to a Higher Power that can do for me something I never could do for myself.

If I use the idea of a heart transplant, it can go some way to helping us understand the dynamic. Firstly, the old heart must be diagnosed as being seriously deficient, and not capable of preserving life. Secondly, a compatible heart must be found, and inserted, in the hope that the system will not reject the new organ, and life can continue to be sustained. It is literally true to say that, by myself, I do not have what it takes to live the Christian life. All of my basic instincts are fundamentally opposed to the very idea of the daily dyings that are part of Christian service. Self-preservation and self-advancement are basic human instincts, and only a higher power can lift me above the quicksand of my own selfishness. I can try all the cosmetic jobs in the world, I can use all the gimmicks and the guidelines of all the behavioural sciences, and there is no way I can improve my human condition. All human attempts to improve the human condition is like mixing water with water, where I will always, and can only, end up with water.

There was a crow that had all his friends worried about him, because he seemed to be very worried and anxious, and was seen to be wasting away before their eyes. One day some of his friends came to him to enquire what it was that was bothering him, and to ask if they might be able to help in any way. At first the crow was embarrassed, but, with much assurance from his friends, he decided to tell them what was troubling him so much.

He felt that life was passing him by, and he seemed to be no nearer now to fulfiling some of his earlier ambitions than he had ever been. When pressed to share what those ambitions might be, he confessed that one of his great ambitions in life was to make a record of himself singing. This evoked a smothered giggle from his listeners, something that hurt him, and caused him to launch into a tirade about how reasonable his ambition was, and it was not something to be laughed at. 'Did you ever hear a blackbird singing? Well, I'm the colour of a blackbird, and I'm bigger, so why couldn't I sing like a blackbird?'

He began to tell them the amount of effort he had put into the task of being able to sing like a blackbird. He had gone to a health shop to buy whole-wheat grain. He bought all the vitamins he could find, and he went on every bio-energy diet available, but all to no avail. After all his efforts, he flew up on a tree, and tried to sing, but all he could produce was a loud 'Caw!'

He then bought a tape-recorder and a c-90 tape, and he flew up among the blackbirds, and filled the tape with the sounds of the blackbirds singing. He then bought a walkman (a brain bypass?!), and as he flew around during the day, he listened to the singing, fully expected that, through some subliminal way, the sounds would be transmitted to him. Once again, however, he flew up on a tree to test his efforts, and once again, all he could produce was a loud 'Caw!'

He was very very discouraged, naturally, but he was determined to carry on. He bought sheet music, and he began to take voice-training lessons. He worked hard at this, in the hope that now, at last, he had found a method that would work. However, he soon found out that his best efforts could not improve on the loud 'Caw!'

His friends listened with growing sympathy and understanding, even though they were amazed to think that he could ever have hoped to be able to sing like a blackbird, without having the voice-box of a blackbird. They hadn't the heart to tell him this, and they just promised to meet again the following day, when they could listen to him at greater length.

The next morning the crow was returning from his early morning fly (he was a keep-fit addict as well!), when he collected the morning paper, and began to browse through it. Something at the bottom of page two caught his eye. It spoke of a surgeon in South Africa named Christian Bernard who did heart transplants. This caused the crow to gasp with excitement at the prospects raised by this information. He rushed home, got on the phone, and in a matter of moments, he was talking to Christian Bernard. He could not contain the excitement in his voice. 'Hello! I see here that you do heart transplants. Do you do any other kind of transplants?' 'Well, we do lung and kidney transplants also, of course'. 'Did you ever do a voice-box transplant?' asked the crow, with mounting excitement. 'Well, not actually, but it wouldn't be any more difficult than a heart transplant'. 'If I went out there, would you do a voice-box transplant for me?' asked the crow, in some sort of whispered plea. 'Yes, of course' came the reply. 'Come on out, and we'll see what we can do'.

The crow immediately set off for South Africa (without even taking time to inform his friends of the previous day). They were in touch with the local hospitals and mortuaries, waiting for some blackbird to keel over (especially one with a donor card!). Eventually, a voice-box became available, and, at last, the poor old crow just lay back, and let somebody else take over, who knew what he was doing, and he had his own voice-box removed, and the voice-box of the blackbird implanted. NOW the crow has what it takes! But, as St Paul advises, even when we have the Holy Spirit, we have 'to learn to live and to walk with the Spirit'. In no time at all, the crow was up on a tree, singing his heart out, as good as any blackbird could ever sing!

It is obvious to us now, just as it was to the crow, when he returned home, that all previous efforts to sing like a blackbird were bound to end up in failure, because there is no way he could do something that was completely outside his natural competence. Upon further reflection, the crow must come to accept that all its efforts up till then were not a waste of time and money, because it was necessary to have tried all those methods, if only to become completely convinced that they just were not capable of working.

Many good people can spend a life-time of effort trying to do something that is beyond their capability. If Jesus thought that we could live the Christian life by ourselves, he would not have thought it necessary to join us on the journey. Only God can do God-things, and living with the life of the Spirit is very definitely a work of God. In non-theological language, I might compare the Holy Spirit to Popeye's spinach!

The prophet Ezekiel spoke these words to the people, on behalf of God 'When you have come back to me ... I will give you a new heart; I will put a new spirit in you. Yes, I will remove their heart of stone, and give them a heart of flesh, that they may walk in my statutes, observe my laws, and practice them, and they shall be my people, and I will be their God.'

Spirit of God, I look to you as the transplant surgeon! I certainly need a transplant, and this is something that only you can do. With all my heart, I wish to open my whole being to the transforming power of your presence. Fill my heart, my mind, my spirit with the inspirations of new life. Stir up within me a whole new enthusiasm for life, and enkindle within me the fires of divine love. Amen.

14. Holding hands together

When Jesus ascended into heaven, he brought the body he had with him. He would send his Spirit, and it would now be up to us to provide the body. A spirit, good or bad, cannot actually do anything, because it needs a voice to tell the lie, a finger to pull the trigger, or a hand to raise up the down-trodden. In a way, all of us, as children of God, are united in the vocation and the person of Mary, the mother of Jesus. She was asked if she would agree to provide the body in which God would dwell, and through which he would effect our salvation. We, in our turn, as her common family, are asked if we are willing to accept the exact same responsibility.

St Paul never actually met Jesus in the flesh, because he was very definitely on the other side of things, while Jesus walked the roads of Galilee. However, when he was blasted off his horse on the road to Damascus, as he went in pursuit of Christians, and he heard the words 'I am Jesus, whom you are persecuting', he had impressed on his mind a very simple and central truth: Jesus considers his followers and himself as being synonymous. From then on, Paul had a very clear concept of the Christian community as the Body of Christ, and all of us are members. In the divine economy of things, we all need each other. Again, to quote from Paul "The body has not just one member, but many. Even though the foot says, 'I do not belong to the body for I am not a hand', it continues to be part of the body. Even though the ear says 'I do not belong to the body, for I am not an eye', it continues to be part of the body. If all the body were an eye, how would you hear? And if all the body were an ear, how would you smell? God has arranged all the members, placing each part of the body as he pleased. If all were the same part where would the body be? But there are many members and one body. The eye cannot tell the hand 'I do not need you', nor the head tell the feet 'I do not need you'."

This story of a little child is supposed to have happened somewhere in South Dakota. The child wandered away from the
house one night. It was dark, wet, and dirty, and there was a
door open, and the child was but a toddler. He could have been
gone for an hour or more before his mother missed him. She
called him, thinking he was watching television. When he
wasn't there, she presumed he was up to something, and that
was why he was keeping so quiet. Anyhow, it was some time
before she realised that, in fact, he was not in the house, and it
was then she noticed that the back door was open.

She ran out the back, calling his name at the top of her voice. It
was a miserable night, and the house was surrounded by wheat
fields, now in full growth, which stretched away to the horizon.
She phoned down to the farm-yard, where her husband was
doing some carpentry work, but, no, the little lad hadn't arrived
down there. They quickly got a search party together, and,
armed with torch lights, they went out into the fields. It was
hours later before they had to abandon the search, with the
intention of resuming with the first light of day.

Some hours later, with the help of neighbours and friends, the
search of the fields began again. People were running in all
directions, searching under trees, in streams, and all the farm
houses. Finally, one man called them all together. He pointed
out that the child was so small, and the wheat was so tall, and
they were running all over the place, without any pattern,
organisation, or fixed purpose to their searching. All of this
could mean that, at any one moment, they could be but a few
feet from the child, and yet not notice him. He asked them to
form a straight line, to hold hands, and to move along the field
in unison, and with unity of purpose.

They did this, and about one hundred yards from the house they
found the child, now in an unconscious state, after being
exposed to the elements all night. It appears he had slipped into
a gully, and was knocked out, and so he had remained there.
Anyhow, they picked him up, and ran towards the house, where
they placed him in his mother's arms. Alas, it was too late,
because just then the last little flicker of life was snuffed, and the
mother knew that her child was dead. She sat on the front steps,

while neighbours and friends looked on helplessly. Then she looked up at them, and from somewhere within her came the cry 'In God's name, in God's name why didn't you people hold hands sooner?'

There is a vast difference between unity and We can be very united, while continuing to be very different people. The force that unites us is the Holy Spirit, and the Spirit is seen at work whenever people come together to share a common purpose for good. If I pray for something, I believe that I am heard. I do not automatically expect that God will give me what I ask. If God were cruel he would give us everything we ask, and then he'd have a good laugh. When I join up with others, and when we pray with one mind and with one heart, then that is a very powerful prayer. It is prayer like this that brings peace, and prevents disasters. I often feel we do not appreciate the power of prayer to change things. And prayer can and does change things.

'In God's name, why didn't you people hold hands sooner?' I often think that many a mother, whose child was killed in violence in this country, or any other country, could say those very same words to us. Peace could have come much sooner, if we had come together sooner to pray as a united community for that peace. It is this concept of power in the unity of the body that gives meaning and purpose to the very idea of church. The church is made up of people, and, hopefully, of people who share a common Spirit, and, therefore, a common vision.

The Holy Spirit is never given to the individual, but to the body, and to the individual only in so far as such a person is part of that body. The Christian community is like a mirror which is taken off a wall, shattered, and a piece given to each of the group. The purpose of community is to invite each one to contribute whatever part of the shattered mirror that is entrusted to each, so that, when the task is done, then we can reflect the face of God. Another image is to think of a situation where I take parts of the engine of a car, and give a part to each person in the group. Unless you are willing to supply the part that you hold, the car cannot work. God gives me nothing for myself, and no one of us is an island, but we are all part of the mainland of humanity. 'Am I my brother's keeper?' is a question that was asked very early in the human journey. Everything that God has said since would give a very definite 'Yes' to that question.

As far back in my life as I can remember, there were groups of people praying for the conversion of Russia, for peace in the world, and, more recently, for peace here at home. Those who organise, inspire, and generate such corporate prayer are, indeed, very much into the work of God's Spirit. Unlike the loss of the child in the story, these are life-giving and life-preserving people, who heed the word of the Lord, who came that we should have life, and have it to the full.

Lord Jesus, through you, the Father reached out a hand of love and friendship to us, so that we, in turn, could reach out to each other. Please fill my heart with your love, so that I willingly reach out to those nearest me, irrespective of colour, creed, or race. Help me open my hands and my heart to all your people. Amen.

15. Always some other time

There is nothing more powerful than an idea whose time has come. On the other hand, there's nothing more destructive than ideas which remain at that stage, and never come to anything. The road to hell is paved with good intentions. God is creator, and creation is something that is on-going, just as love is constantly seeking new ways of expression. People with bright or good ideas, but who never get around to doing anything with them, or about them, are certainly not life-giving people. They are drones in the hive of God's people, and they draw from the Lord a very harsh comment indeed 'I wish that you were hot or cold. but, because you are luke-warm, I will begin to vomit you out of my mouth.' In other words, you make me sick, says God, because that is what any of us would do with anything that made us sick.

A little girl was seated at the kitchen table, with a sheet of paper, a pencil, and a box of paints. 'What are you drawing?' asked her mother. 'I'm drawing a picture of God', was the reply. The mother smiled, and said 'But, darling, nobody knows what God looks like', to which the child replied, with total conviction 'Ah, yes, mammy, but they will know what God looks like when I'm finished!' There is something beautiful in that little story about attempting the impossible. God loves a trier, and he promises peace on earth to those of good-will. Someone said one time that, when all is said and done, there's much more said than done!

There is a story about a meeting in hell, where the daddy devil rounded up all his forces, to review recent developments in the world, and to up-date some of the tactics being used. He was particularly concerned about programmes of renewal, and the re-emergence of spirituality, as opposed to religion. Generally speaking, he never felt very threatened by religion, because that

tended to have a human base, to be propelled with human
effort, to be about control, and with a strong emphasis on externals, and how things appeared on the outside. He was genuinely concerned about spirituality, because that was a totally different thing entirely. That is about surrender, it is about the heart,
and is something that only God can effect. That was a cause of
real concern for him. As long as humans relied on their own
efforts, he would continue to out-manoeuvre them every time.
However, through spiritual living, where God is in charge, and
the person gets out of the way, that could cause serious damage
to the work of his troops here among us.

The daddy devil walked up and down in front of the assembled
multitude, and it was quite obvious that this was going to be a
very important meeting. He spoke to them at great length about
his concerns, and his worries for the future. He spoke of how
dramatically things have changed over the years, and, because
of modern communication, there was a growing concern among
people about global issues, like hunger, injustice, and pollution.
He spoke about his real concern with the steps for renewal and
updating taking place among the Christian churches. He went
on and on, detailing the many many reasons he had for being
quite concerned, and genuinely worried.

He stopped pacing the floor, and he looked straight at the
group, as he asked them to put on their thinking caps, to come
up with some ingenious plan that would put them firmly back
in business for the remainder of this century. He spoke of the
urgency of the situation, and how necessary it was to have a
plan ready for implementation as soon as possible.

There was silence all around the room, as each was lost in
thought and reflection. Finally, the spell was broken when one
little devil put up his hand, and was called forward to give his
contribution. 'I suggest we go up there, and tell them there's no
such place as hell! That way, they will see no reason why they
should avoid evil, and so we will catch them that way.' All his
pals loudly applauded this suggestion, which seemed so simple,
and so easy to put into effect. The daddy devil pondered the
idea for a while, and then he shook his head. 'No, no', he said,
'that just wouldn't work. If you know anything at all about

human nature, you would realise that that idea would never sell. Humans are strange creatures. One look at a child of two, and the mother knows rightly that he has been up to something! There is some sort of inner mechanism within them that monitors their behaviour, and every person knows only too well when behaviour merits reward or punishment. No, no, no, … that will not do. Come on, get back to using your intelligence, and give me an idea that will work.'

There a further long silence, as each was seen to be in deep reflection. Then, again, another little devil raised his hand, and was called forward to share his suggestion. 'I suggest we go up and tell them that there is a hell, but there's no such place as heaven. That way, they will see no point in doing good, because there is nothing but damnation awaiting them at the end, and so we will catch them all in the net of despair.' At that, all his pals applauded this suggestion with great enthusiasm. The daddy devil thought about that for a while. Then, once again, he shook his head, and said 'No, no, that would never work', he thundered. 'If you know anything about humans, you must know that there is some sort of resilience in the human heart that causes them to hope and expect that tomorrow will be better, no matter how bad things are today. No, no, they would just never buy that one.' Once again, he harangued them at some length, telling them the urgency of the situation, and how he desperately needed a plan right now, one that would boost their results, and that would carry them over well into the next century.

Another silence descended on the gathering, and it was obvious that each was desperately trying to come up with something original, and something that would have the desired effect. Genius is the ability to discern the obvious, and most of them knew that there just had to be a plan that was so simple, that they were not seeing it. Eventually, one little devil raised his hand, and, as with the others, he was ushered to the podium to present his suggestion. 'Why don't we go up and tell them that there is a hell, and there is a heaven. However, we could try to get them to believe that there was no urgency about this whole question, and that there was no need to bother about any serious decision-making about those options for now, because this was something they could think about some other time.' The daddy devil thought about that for all of one second. Then he walked up to the speaker, shook his hand warmly, and announced 'That's it! That's it! We have it! If you go up there now, and tell them that there is a hell, and there is a heaven, but that there's no hurry; that next Monday, New Year's Day, next Lent, when the kids are reared, when they retire, anything, but anything, that will succeed in delaying any decision, that will distract them from doing anything about their options, that's our trump card! All we need for evil to succeed is that good people should do nothing! That's brilliant! And it's such a simple idea! There is no scarcity of ideas up there, but there is nothing scares me as much as a good idea whose time has come! In our line of business, we have constant proof that the road to here is paved with good intentions! Please, please, try to keep them in their heads, because we can out-play them there. Please don't let them down into their hearts, because that is where truth abides, and if they get in touch with truth, we're in serious trouble! I believe that we now have a programme, not just for the turn of the century, but for as long as there are humans out there to conquer.' Have you heard that whisper lately?!

'Procrastination is the thief of time' is a wise and true saying. All diets start on Monday, and there are many many people out there who are going to stop smoking, or give up alcohol next Lent! There is a serious problem with this sort of thinking. 'Now is the acceptable time. Today is the day of salvation.' The moment of grace is always now! How often do we read in the gospel where 'Jesus of Nazareth is passing by.' Supposing the blind man of Jericho thought along these or similar lines: 'I know I want to see, but I'm not sure I want to do so just now. I think I'll let Jesus go on his way, and I'll ask him to drop by again some other day.' What is to prevent him thinking along those same lines on the next occasion as well? Jesus met a man who had missed out on moments of grace over a period of thirty-eight years, and his opening question was very very pointed: 'Do you want to be healed?'

There are three groups of people in any society. There are those who cause things to happen, those who watch things happening, and those who haven't a clue what's happening! Satan is not at all threatened by thinkers, by people who live up in their heads. They have no sense of urgency, and their tendency to be cautious and prudent about everything will slow them down to being effectively inactive. On the other hand, Satan has every good reason to be threatened by the doer, because such a one will always be highly effective in doing good, and, because there is little delay between the decision and the carrying out of it, Satan has much less time to distract, or to suggest alternative actions. There is a wholesome aggression about such people, and all dilly-dallying is just swept aside. 'Enthusiasm' comes from the Greek 'theos', meaning God, and it literally means to have God within. Because God is totally a God of now, then one can expect an enthusiastic person to be some-one who does now what another would leave off till some other time. There are some people who cannot see why they should do something today, if it can be put off till tomorrow!

Spirit of God, I turn to you as a Spirit of truth. So often, I make excuses, and I put off something that should be done now. You must surely see this as another form of lie, deceit, injustice. Please strengthen resolve, and help me become a person of action, someone who, while dreaming dreams, is prepared to pay the price to make the dreams come true. Amen.

16. And God created mothers

Scientists now tell us that we are all conceived as female for the first twenty-seven days. Between then and the thirty-sixth day some of the embryos become male, while the others continue as female. This is an interesting insight, because it highlights something that is quite often overlooked, or simply ignored. There is a feminine dimension in all men, as there is a masculine side to all women. Wholeness is achieved when that other side is acknowledged and developed. The idea that 'Irish men don't cry' is most pathetic, if it is true, and it certainly doesn't flatter the men concerned. When a man develops the feminine in him, when he is open to developing within him all the characteristics for loving and caring that he sees displayed by his wife towards her children, then he has become more complete as a man.

It would be both wrong and inaccurate to dismiss attempts at emphasising the feminine in God as being some sort of aberration of feminism. Far from it. If God is love, which we believe him to be, then he must combine within himself all that is best in both male and female. He must have the heart that has all the qualities of a male and female heart. There must be a fullness and a completeness about God's love, in which all grades and levels of authentic human love is reflected. Some of us were blessed from early infancy with the love of two parents, and this is the best possible preparation for coming into an acceptance of God's love in later life. The following little parable about how God created mothers gives a whimsical view of the way God might have been thinking, as he created a creature whose very nature is to love. A mother's love is something that is deeply instinctual, that is part of who she is. A mother's love is proverbial, and, I would strongly contend, it is totally impossible to come to any sense of God's love, unless I can understand the love in the heart of a mother.

When the good Lord was creating mothers, he was into his sixth day of overtime. An angel appeared and said 'You're doing a lot of fiddling around on this one.' And the Lord said, 'Have you read the specifications on this order? She has to be completely washable, but not plastic ... have 180 movable parts, all replaceable ... run on black coffee and left-overs ... have a lap that disappears when she stands up ... a kiss that can cure anything from a broken leg to a disappointed love affair ... and six pairs of hands.' The angel shook her head slowly and said 'Six pairs of hands? No way.' 'It's not the hands that are causing me problems,' said the Lord. 'It's the three pairs of eyes that mothers have to have.' 'That's on the standard model?' asked the angel. The Lord nodded. 'One pair that sees through closed doors when she asks 'What are you children doing in there?', when she already knows. Another in the back of her head that sees what she shouldn't see, but what she needs to know. And, of course, the ones in front that can look at a child when he gets himself into trouble, and say 'I understand, and I love you', without so much as uttering a word.'

'Lord,' said the angel, touching his sleeve gently, 'go to bed. Tomorrow is another....' 'I can't,' said the Lord. 'I'm so close now. Already I have one who heals herself when she is sick, can feed a family of six on one pound of mince, and can even get a nine-year-old to have a bath.' The angel circled the model of the mother very slowly. 'It's too soft,' she sighed. 'But tough!' said the Lord excitedly. 'You cannot imagine what this mother can do or endure.' 'Can it think?' 'Not only think, but it can reason and compromise,' said the Lord. Finally, the angel bent over and ran her finger across the cheek. 'There's a leak.' she whispered. 'It's not a leak,' said the Lord. 'It's a tear.' 'What's that for?' 'It's for joy, sadness, disappointment, pain, loneliness and pride.' 'You're a genius,' said the angel. The Lord looked at her seriously for a moment, and whispered, 'It wasn't I who put that tear there.'

I remember seeing a poster of a grandmother, deep in thought, and the thought was in a circle up over her head, 'I love my grandchildren, and now I'm really sorry I didn't have them first!' Just as a mother is the source of great and special love, so she also needs that love to be returned, to sustain her in her own life. Unselfish love from mothers, love that is not always appreciated or returned, is proverbial. However, we are all human, and, with King Lear, many a parent could say 'How sharper than a serpent's tooth it is to have a thankless child.' A son or daughter who fails to appreciate the love of a good parent, who takes such for granted, as something that is theirs by right; worse still who takes advantage of the generosity of a parent's love, … such a one is most to be pitied. I remember an Arab guide in the Holy Land telling me than it was part of their teaching and of their belief that, by taking good care of one's own parents, one was ensuring that similar care would be available to them when their turn came to be dependent upon others.

It is interesting to note that the first three commandments have to do directly with God, while the very next one speaks of honouring our parents. God has arranged things in such a way that any proper (if limited) understanding of him is tied in closely with the idea of God as parent. Now, obviously, I allow full space and recognition for Mary, the mother of Jesus, in any consideration of the feminine side of God's love. However, I must insist on a further distinction, in considering the love of God. Mary had only one mother, human or divine, that she was aware of, and that was Anne. Yet, more than any other human being, she must have had a profound and awesome awareness of God's love. To her, this love would have been so all-embracing that she would surely accept that it contained, within itself, every possible expression of sincere human love there is. This would surely include the highest form of human love known to us, the love of a father and a mother for a child.

I believe that reflection on the story offered in this chapter will greatly help us in getting further insight into the great love of God. I remember one time being asked by a group of kids if God had a sense of humour, and, with tongue in cheek, I replied, 'A sense of humour? You should come with me to see some of the people he created, and you'll be fully convinced that he has quite a sense of humour!' On a serious note, however, the more human love I witness, the more loving people I encounter, the more God's love is made real to me. Because I am a mere human, I can only go from the known to the unknown, and my starting point is my own experiential knowledge.

By way of concluding this reflection, I will add a short story that can help elaborate on this same theme. A young mother had to go out of the house for a short while, and she asked her two children to set the table for dinner while she was out, and to switch on the oven at a certain time. When she returned, she was delighted to see that the table was set, and the smell of cooking from the oven confirmed that that job had also been attended to. She was just about to go into the front room to thank the children, when she noticed a piece of paper on the table. She picked it up, read it, and was deeply hurt and shocked by what it contained: 'For setting the table £2, for switching on the oven £1. Total £3. Please pay now.' She was unsure if it was a practical joke, or a very selfish idea. She got a large sheet of paper and a pen, and she began to write with gusto: 'For carrying you in the womb, for giving you life, for preserving that life through many illnesses; for the food that you eat, and the clothes on your back; for the toys, the birthdays, the vacations; for a thousand other things … the bill is NOTHING.' The mother then placed the sheet of paper on the table, and left the house for a walk around the block, making sure the children knew she was after going back out again. When she returned she was met with apologies and tears, and her children had learned a simple if fundamental lesson.

Mary my Mother, you are a very special gift to me from Jesus just before he died. You have a mother's heart, and we are asked to be like children before God. You did perfectly what we're trying to do, in our own fumbling, bumbling way. I look to you, and to the love in your heart, to stand with us, to stay with us, to pray with us, and to pray for us, that we may, more and more, come into full membership in the family of God. Amen.

17. God's gifts are free

For people who were reared on religion, the idea of earning or meriting salvation is something that was part of the package that was passed onto them. God kept records, everything was noted and recorded, and, at the final judgement, the books are balanced, and the result is announced. God was seen as being more interested in justice than in love. He would have the final laugh, as he exacted his pound of flesh.

In explaining where this kind of religion came from, St Paul, in his letter to the Romans tells how Moses had announced that, if a person was totally faithful to the law, with all its ramifications, had neither sinned nor yielded to temptation even once, that such a person was saved. One is tempted to ask 'Saved from what, and for what?' St Paul then goes on to stress that such observance is impossible and unnecessary. This thinking and teaching produced the Pharisees, who were completely taken up with the observance of law. In the parable Jesus told about the Pharisee in the temple, he has him telling God just how good he is, and how faithful he is to all the rules and ordinances of his religion. He then goes that one logical step further, when he compares himself to the publican, who is not as virtuous as he, and, therefore, by implication, not as deserving of God's love and approval. There is always the risk of great disillusionment, when religious people are told that God is more interested in weighing their prayers, than in counting them! God is more into quality than quantity. He is more into the disposition of the heart than external actions. Such actions, if only external, and not the outcome of a sincere heart, are but 'sounding brass and clanging cymbal'. In my own life-time, I grew up with a spirituality of addition, where the idea was to add on more and more prayers. Thankfully, I now am moving, more and more, into the spirituality of subtraction! The more I can succeed in getting out of the way, the more freedom the Lord has in my life.

When Jesus wanted to emphasise the kind of openness needed for proper understanding and acceptance of his message, he chose a very simple example, i.e., the heart of a child. 'Unless you become like little children ...'. I have never yet met a child who was in any way reluctant to let the whole world know that 'to-morrow's my birthday'! Children take free gifts for granted. The most selfish individual in a family is a new-born baby, who, essentially, is constantly saying 'feed me, change me, nurse me', and yet that baby is the most loved in the family. In normal circumstances, children are reared to trust that their needs will be taken care of. Santa is always reliable, birthdays are always honoured, and granny always brings something when she visits. Jesus is making a very strong, and a very important point, when he insists that we relate best to God, whom Jesus calls Abba (literally, 'Daddy'), when we approach with the heart of a child.

It is a Thursday night, the night the family visits the local supermarket to do the weekly shopping. There is mam, dad, and junior, aged six. Because of experience, they don't need a list. They move from aisle to aisle, picking, choosing, selecting. It is a fairly routine and predictable chore, with the exception of the few 'special deals' that always seem to appear from time to time. In no time at all the trolley is full, and it is time to head towards the check-out to assess the damage! The father begins putting the goods on the conveyor belt, while the mother gets a second trolley, into which she will transfer the goods, once they have been itemised. A young shop assistant approaches, and takes her place in front of the cash register. Then she turns to the father, and says 'Today, everything is free; there is no charge.' This draws a benign smile from the father, as he continues to transfer goods onto the conveyor belt. Of course, he has a sense of humour, and he can recognise the ridiculous, when he sees it, just as much as anyone else. He is also a sharp thinker, and he instinctively peeps around in search of someone from a 'Candid Camera' crew. He checks the identity tag the girl is wearing, just to make sure that she actually is a member of staff here.

There is a gradual heightening of temperature, as he continues to place the groceries on the conveyor belt, and the girl continues to insist that all is free! Maybe she has had a row with her boss, and this is her way of getting back at him? I wonder is that man over there a store detective, just watching to see what's going to happen? As his frustration mounts, he swears that this is the last time he's going to come into this place. In the meantime, where is Junior? He heard the magic word 'free', and he responded immediately. He grabbed another trolley, and he's now flying down the aisles, filling it as fast as he can with all the things he loves! He has none of the problems that are driving his poor dad demented!

This is a story that merits reflection. I cannot over-stress that salvation, love, acceptance, and all that we receive from God is pure gift. There is no way I can earn it, or become 'good enough' to merit it. There are basic conditions required on my side of the equation, of course. Without putting them in any particular order, I must be convinced that I need them, that there is no way I can earn them, and that they become mine, if I trust God enough to deliver on his promises. The gap between human and divine is so wide that I cannot cross it, I cannot come to him, I cannot raise myself above my condition. I depend totally on Incarnation, where God comes to where I am, and he does for me what I never could do for myself.

Humility has had a bad press over the years. Having being reared on a 'children should be seen and not heard' philosophy, and where parents and teachers were very sparing with praise, because 'you might get a swelled head', one could easily confuse humility with an acceptance of inadequacy or uselessness. Nothing could be further from the truth. 'God don't make no junk!' was one man's way of answering that one. (Thank God, things have changed today! I saw a notice the other day, advocating that children should wear reflector arm-bands in the winter, and it said 'Children should be seen, and not hurt'.) I am a central part of God's creation. At each stage of creation we are told that 'God saw that it was good.' So good, in fact, that God designed his human creation to be raised to the fullness of life, and to have an eternal quality. And that is total gift, and is away beyond any or all of us.

For a few years, I worked in a parish. I have happy memories of that time, and especially happy memories of the children. On Christmas morning there was a steady stream to the front door, while I stood there 'oozing' awe and amazement at all the wonderful things Santa had brought! And then, on a regular basis, during the rest of the year, there were constant little callers to tell me 'To-morrow is my birthday!' Hint, hint! I never ceased to be impressed by the freedom and innocence they displayed at such times, and I always saw this as being part of the heart of a child that Jesus speaks of. Those same children will lose all of that in the not-too-distant future, and, indeed, some of them might get so hide-bound by convention that, when they are in great need later on, they just cannot accept assistance from anyone. Some of them carry this need for some sort of false independence (pride?) throughout their lives. The most human people I have known have been among the very young, and the very old! Somewhere in between, we seem to lose the vision and the dream.

Humility before God is simply a willingness to accept things as they are, which results from the work of God's Spirit, the Spirit of truth, in my heart. Jesus said that his Spirit would lead us into all truth, and that then we would be free. Coming to a conviction that God's gifts are free does not mean that I become irresponsible, and take God and his gifts for granted. It would be hoped and expected that an openness to such love and generosity would generate a totally different response from within my heart. Here I think of the spirit of Mary's prayer of praise and thanks, when she sang 'He that is mighty has done great things for me, and holy is his name.' Mary magnified the Lord, she didn't put herself down. If I am to take my proper place before God, then the bigger my God, the more obvious my place will be. The bigger my God, the smaller my problems. Some people have very big problems, because their God is far too small. We speak of Mary having a mother's heart. It would be worth reflecting on the child's heart she displayed in her trust and submission to God. Part of being a child is to have that sense of awe and wonder in the presence of mystery and the unexplainable.

St Therese of Lisieux provides a wonderful example of someone with the heart of a child, and with the attitude of a child, when it comes to God. She had this strong conviction that she wanted to be a saint, and she simply concluded that God would not put that desire in her heart without supplying all that it took to make that a reality. And so, she expected to be a saint, and she said so very definitely before she died. She spoke of herself as a toddler trying to climb onto the bottom step of a stairs, only to fall back to the floor each time. Eventually, God, her Father, came down the stairs, took her in his arms, and carried her to the top. And that was how she was going to become a saint. And that is just exactly how it happened.

> *Lord, you know us through and through. You know exactly what it is in us that insists on retaining part or full control of things, and makes us unwilling to let go. Lord, I have no reason to trust myself, and I don't even want to be in charge of the letting-go! I just present my willingness to you, and I trust your Spirit to make full and proper use of all that I am, so that I may be enabled to get out of the way, and know my place. Amen.*

18. Give it all away

God gives me nothing for myself. He doesn't give me the gift of speech to go around talking to myself! From the early days of the Church the charismatic dimension was strongly emphasised. A charisma is a gift, but it is a gift for others. The gifts of the Spirit were charismatic gifts, because they were given for the building up of the church. Jesus tells the story of the coins to teach us about the use of the gifts we receive from God. (Mt 25:14-30)

The person with five thousand coins invested them, and gained five thousand more. He was commended by his master for acting wisely. The person with two thousand coins invested them, and gained two thousand more, and was also commended for the good use he had made of the gifts entrusted to me. The person with one thousand coins considered that it wasn't worth his while trying to do anything with so little, so he buried his treasure in the ground to keep it safe for his master's return. This servant was strongly condemned for his neglect, and even what he had was taken from him, and given to another. This same parable is recounted in slightly different ways in three of the four Gospels. Generally the word talent is used for the kind of riches entrusted for investment. This word later came to mean a gift or an ability to do something well. A leading psychologist recently stated that most people live their lives, and discover only about one quarter of the gifts they have been given in life.

One time there was an old tramp who heard that the King of Kings was coming to a certain village. He didn't know what that might mean, but, with a title like that, he must surely be a man of great importance, and, possibly, of great wealth. He headed off to the village, in the hope of getting to meet such an important person. In his heart he considered this a golden opportunity to

79

try for a little alms, knowing that, for such a wealthy person, a fist of money wouldn't even be missed.

He arrived in the village, only to discover that every other tramp in the countryside had arrived as well! He made enquiries, and was told that, yes, he would get an opportunity to meet the King of Kings. He would, however, have to stand in line, and await his turn. It was the following afternoon before his turn came. As he entered the building his mind was racing with all the things he was going to ask for. He had a list made out, lest the first items were refused.

Finally, he was in the presence of the great man. Before he got a word out of his mouth, the King of Kings said to him, 'And, you, what do you have for me?' He was totally taken aback, as he stuttered, 'Me ... ee... ee? I don't have anything for you.' 'But you must have something', the king replied. 'Everybody has something to give and to offer to others.' 'Well, I have nothing', said the tramp, with great annoyance. The king insisted. 'Of course, you have something to give. Don't expect me to believe that you have nothing.' The tramp was really angry now. By way of insult, rather than generosity, he reached into a pocket, took out a handkerchief, in which he carried some ears of grain for chewing as he walked along the road. He picked out two little gains, and, with total sarcasm in his attitude, he solemnly handed them to the king. The king thanked him for the grains, as he turned and walked away!

The tramp was furious. He stomped out the door, and pounded his way down the road, muttering to himself with rage and frustration. He felt cheated, rejected, belittled, and a whole storm of different emotions welled up inside him. He had gone about a mile, when, as if by instinct, he pulled out the handkerchief to get a few grains to chew. As his fingers dipped into the grains, he was totally amazed and 'gobsmacked' to see two tiny grains of gold among the grains of corn. The reality of what had happened hit him like a sledge hammer. He thumped his forehead in complete disgust, as he muttered 'You fool! Why didn't you give them all away!'

Is it possible that when I die, everything I kept for myself in life will die with me? I am not implying that I should always be giving, in the sense that every moment, and every effort of my life should be spent in the service of others! If I were to do that, and have nothing for myself, either by way of time or attention, I would soon have nothing to give others. The story is told about Carl Jung, the world-famous psycho-analyst, and a titled lady who lived in the same area. She contacted Jung, looking for an appointment on a Wednesday afternoon, stressing that it was very important, and this was the only time that really suited her. Jung explained that he was unable to meet her that afternoon, because of a very important previous appointment in his diary. The lady tried to bully, cajole, and coax him into cancelling his other appointment in favour of her, but he was inflexible, and he held out very definitely. On the Wednesday afternoon, as the lady was being chauffeur-driven along the sea-front, she was very surprised, and very angry, to see Jung strolling along the beach, all by himself! The following morning she came striding into his office, with high-pitched voice, and pointed finger, as she accused him of being a liar, and of deceiving her about his appointment of the previous afternoon. Jung heard her out, and then quietly replied, 'Madam, I did have an appointment yesterday afternoon. In fact, I have a permanent appointment every Wednesday afternoon. That appointment is with myself, and I always keep it, because if I don't, I'll have nothing to offer to others when I keep my appointments with them.'

What I mean, when I speak of giving to others, has to do with the gifts God has given me for others. We are all gifted by God in a unique and special way. I remember trying to demonstrate this one day in a class of second-level students. I gave one hundred pennies to five different pupils, and asked that they divide these in any way each wished, in whatever number of pockets each possessed. One put fifty in two pockets. Another put twenty-five in four pockets. Another even boasted that he put ten in ten pockets. Of course, the idea of the exercise was to show them that, no matter what each did with the pennies, they were all worth only a pound! Some were gifted in certain areas, while being hopeless in other areas. I have come across pupils in school who were wizards at science or languages, but who couldn't boil an egg! On the other hand, I have seen pupils who were almost illiterate when it came to languages, but were pure geniuses at woodwork, metalwork, or home economics.

God gives me my quota of riches from his store-house. I do not, nor can I, discover what those riches are. If I do, I am like someone at a party who insists on singing, while being the only person present who thinks he/she can sing! On the other hand, there is someone at the same party, and everyone is calling on her/him to sing! This is where the gift is evident! I myself, I who write these words, have been asked to give Retreats, etc., and, even if I protest my inadequacy, I just cannot allow a false humility or a lack of confidence to permit me evade what the Lord is clearly calling me to do. The Lord gives me gifts, and He very clearly indicates what those gifts are by what people expect me to provide. If someone asks me to give a talk, to write an article, or to conduct a Retreat, then I must take that request seriously, and never lightly dismiss it, for no good reason.

It is one of paradoxes of Christianity that 'it is in giving that we receive'. The more I give, the more I receive. If I do not give, even that which I have will be taken away from me. It is sad to finish the journey of life, and, like the tramp in the story, I thump myself on the forehead, and say 'Fool! Why didn't you give it all away?'

Spirit of God, please create a generous heart in me. I am always afraid of the head, where I keep my weighing-scales, and my balance books! In my heart, I would love to be generous, but I depend totally on your inspirations, and on the power to carry out those inspirations. I can just offer you my honest desire to become a giving person, and trust that you will accept that, and make full use of that. Thanks, Lord. Amen.

19. Nobody comes back

Life is a journey from the womb life, through the womb of life, into the fullness of life. I made a video one time called 'Death a Fact of Life'. The opening scene was a film of a birth that I had bought from a television station. The baby was born, the cord was cut, and immediately the scene turned to the straps being pulled up out of a grave, as the coffin was lowered. In this second scene the cord was cut yet again, and life continued in the third and final stage. Life, as we know it, is a journey from one birth to another birth. I once heard the following description of a worthwhile life: When you were born you alone cried, and everybody else was happy. Live your life in such a way that when you die, you will be very happy, and everybody else will be crying!

There is a very wide gap between the three stages of life. Just imagine the situation if the unborn baby could hear your voice clearly. You try to strike up a conversation. There is not one word you could use that the unborn baby would understand. Book, house, weather, family, etc. ... not one word would mean anything to the baby. Now apply this concept to someone who has gone ahead to the next stage of life. If a person came back it would simply be a case of me not being able to understand one thing being said. St Paul tells us that eye has not seen, nor has ear heard, nor has it entered into the heart of people to conceive of what God has prepared for those who love him.

Thomas Aquinas says that whatever I say about God, I can be sure that I am wrong, because He is so much more than that! It is just not possible for us to encapsulate in our puny minds the concept of the infinite. I look at a circle, and consider that that represents the scope of my own personal experience. I then consider that there is an infinity of life and of experience outside the perimeter of that circle. To dismiss anything outside the scope of my own experience would be unpardonable arrogance. Just as the unborn baby cannot possibly have any idea of what the next stage of life will be like, so with me and the stage of life yet to come.

> In the bottom of a lily-pond some grubs were deep in conversation. They were wondering what happened to any of their members who climb the stem of the lilies, and do not return. They agreed among themselves that the next one who would climb the stem of the lily would come back and tell what happened.
>
> Some time later one grub felt drawn by nature to climb the lily-stem to the surface above. He did so in the sure conviction that he would honour his promise, and return to let the others know what happened to him. When he reached the surface, he was amazed. It was so bright and warm up here. It had been so cold and dark below. And then suddenly, something strange and wonderful began happening to him. He began to change shape, to take on a different form, and to emerge as a beautiful dragon-fly, with wings of dazzling brilliance. He never dreamt he would become a dragon-fly, because he thought he was destined to remain a grub for all his existence.
>
> He flew back and forth across the pond, with a burning desire to return to his friends and tell them what had happened. He could see them below, but they couldn't see him. It took him some time to realise that he just could not get back to them. After a while he clearly saw the pointlessness of such an attempt. He was now convinced that, even if they could see him, they would never recognise such a truly beautiful creature as ever being one of them.

Yes, indeed, no one comes back to tell us, and it is just as well, because it would be a futile exercise. The gulf between the three stages of life is vast, and the only valid knowledge has to be experiential. I can have all the theories in the world, and apply my vivid imagination to its limits, and yet not come remotely near to grasping anything of the reality. I myself have produced two booklets, an audio tape, and a video tape on death, and yet I know that I actually have to die first to be able to speak about it with any authority, and with any knowledge.

It is in this area, perhaps, more than most, that our faith in Jesus, and in his promises, is seen at its starkest. When it comes to passing through the Red Sea into the Promised Land, there is no one else who can part the waters for us. His own life and death was a blueprint for all of us. All of our hope of resurrection is based totally on the resurrection of Jesus. The daughter of Jairus, the widow of Naim's son, and Lazarus were brought back to life, and they still had to die. Death was still a reality for them. Jesus, however, passed through death, and came out victoriously at the other end. He spent the next forty days with his disciples, using every possible means to convince them that he was, indeed, alive, and that he had overcome death, the final enemy.

When we speak of Jesus, and what he has done for us, we often speak in the past tense. 'Dying, you destroyed our death. Rising, you restored our life. By your cross and resurrection, you have set us free....' All of this has been done, it is ours already. St Paul links our death and resurrection directly to the death and resurrection of Jesus. 'So then, if you are risen with Christ, seek the things that are above .... For you have died, and your life is now hidden with Christ in God. When Christ, who is our life, reveals himself, you also will be revealed with him in glory.' (Col 3:1-4) Christ has won the victory, and he invites us to claim it. Just as the grub became a dragon-fly, the metamorphosis, or the total change of condition is continually going on in the heart of the Christian. I know I do not have to remain a grub forever! That's the good news of the gospel. I must remember, however, that I don't have to wait till after death for the transformation to begin. Salvation, redemption, resurrection, heaven are now, to be brought to completion when I reach the fulness of life in the next and final stage. I can live with the sure and certain hope. I can live with the expectation of resurrection now. It is a basic characteristic of a Christian to be a person with hope, in the face of the greatest odds.

There is a direct link-up between our faith and our expectations. Our expectations come from our faith. God will never disappoint you. If you don't expect him to answer your prayer, he won't! On the other hand, as Jesus himself tells us, 'If you ask anything in prayer, believing you have received, you have it.' There can be no boundaries to Christian hope. I can close my eyes in death, with the sure and certain hope of opening them to the vision of God for all eternity. Nowhere is faith more stark, and nowhere is love more trusting. To breathe my last with the prayer of Jesus on my lips 'Father, into your hands I commend my spirit' is the supreme act of abandonment, and such trust will be eternally rewarded.

Holy Spirit, Spirit and Breath of God, I need your guiding presence all the way. My human vision is so limited that it is difficult for me to see beyond the immediate. I ask, please, for a strong sense of hope, a hope that holds firm through the journey of life. I don't need to understand much of what lies ahead, but I do need to look forward to it all with great hope. I depend on you for this. Thanks. Amen.

20. God always answers prayer

One young lad asked God (rather than Santa!) for a bicycle. He didn't get the bicycle, and his pal was jeering him about the fact that God hadn't answered his prayer. 'Oh, yes, he did answer my prayer,' replied the other, with quiet conviction. 'It's just that, this time, the answer was NO!' NO is also an answer. If God were sadistic, he would give us everything we ask for, and have a good laugh, because we must surely ask for many things that are not for our own good. God will always give you what you ask, unless he has something better to give you. Prayer is not about trying to manipulate God, trying to put him on the spot, as it were, and have him jumping through hoops at our command! Prayer is an expression of a relationship with God, and, through prayer, I come to know, love, and serve God. The more I come to know God, the more at ease I am with whether he gives me what I ask or not. I come to pray with the mind of Jesus, to use Paul's words, when I conclude each request with the words 'But not my will, but yours be done.' The human will is a dangerous ally, not to be trusted. I would be the last one to know if my will had run riot, and was running the show! If I am honest, I have no reason to trust myself at all, because I cannot possibly know what is best for me. I can be only too aware of what I want, but that may not necessarily be what I need. No one would pretend to believe that a very small child should know what is best to do, what is best to eat, or, in general, what is best for her/him. In God's eyes, his perspective of us must closely resemble how we see very young children.

It is pure common sense that I learn to know my place before God. The creator and the creature, the Saviour and the sinner, the infinite and the human. Jesus spoke of the attitude or the stance taken up by the Pharisee, as he stood before God in the temple. This was much worse than anything he said. Instead of 'Speak, Lord, your servant is listening', it was 'Listen, Lord, your servant is speaking.' Jesus speaks about the servant working in the fields and coming back to the house. Should he expect his master to wait on him at table, or should he rather continue to serve at a different level? Jesus reminds us that the servant is simply doing his duty, is doing what is expected of him. He cannot be spoken of as a profitable servant for doing what he is supposed to be doing. God created us to know, love and serve him, and, when we do this, we are simply doing what we were created to do in the first place, so what credit can we claim? It is in this way that we must always think of salvation, redemption, or heaven as being absolutely pure free gift, not capable of being earned or merited by us in any way. Prayer does not give us any right to have a claim on God! When I speak of prayer being an expression of a relationship with God, I include here all that is best in a healthy relationship. It is not about ownership, or about backing another into some sort of blackmail situation, where our will and wish prevail. Prayer must never degenerate into manipulation. Prayer is so much more than petition, but when it is petition, it simply presents my needs to God, and leaves the manner, timing, and content of the response to him. Prayer, in this way, is an act of trust in God. It should also alert me to the answer, because, at the time, I still do not know what God's answer will be.

> The waters of the dam had burst their banks, and a veritable tidal wave was heading towards the nearest town. The police drove up the main-street with loud speakers, calling on all people to vacate their homes, and to avail of the transport provided for a quick exit out of town. One man, who knew about the danger, refused the offer, because he had prayed to God, and he felt it was now up to God to take care of him. Shortly afterwards the waters came roaring down the main street, and all ground-floors were under water. The man was forced to retreat upstairs. He was at a front window when a boat came by, and the folks in the boat tried to persuade him to join them, as they rowed towards safety. Once again, the man refused, because he still insisted that God would look after him. After some more time the water rose so high that the man was forced to climb out the window and up on the roof. Then a helicopter came along, and

offered to bring him to safety. Once again he refused, as he stub-
bornly waited for God to rescue him. Anyhow, surprise, surprise, he was drowned! He arrived at the gates of heaven in a
very angry and belligerent mood. When he met Peter, he asked
if there was anybody awake up here, and what happens anymore when someone like him asks God for help. This puzzled
Peter, who explained that, yes, God does answer prayers, and
there seemed to be something really odd about this particular
case. He brought out the log-book of prayer, asked the man his
name, and began to check the records. After a while, he looked
up at the man, and said 'Yes, there is a record here of your
prayers. What puzzles me, though, is that there is also a record
here of several answers to those prayers. It says here that we
sent you the police, a group of people in a boat, and we even sent
a helicopter. Whatever happened to all that help? Didn't they
show up?!'

Fundamentalism of any kind is always dangerous, because it is so
tunnel-visioned, and so arrogantly sure of itself. St Paul speaks of
'learning to live and to walk in the Spirit.' There is no learning in
fundamentalism, however, because everything is completely predictable, and entirely under control. Walking in the Spirit has been
compared to riding the wind, like a seagull on a stormy day. The
seagull makes the wind do the work, and is literally as free as a
bird, allowing the currents direct the speed and direction of the
soaring. The fundamentalist ploughs straight ahead, and over-runs
anyone who dares get in the way.

God is infinitely compassionate, tolerant, kind, and patient. When
he is allowed enter into our lives, and effect our behaviour, we, too,
develop some of those divine characteristics. We are freed from the
arrogance of fundamentalism, and we certainly would not ever
want to dictate to God in any way. I open my heart to God, allow
him total access, and leave the rest to him. Religion can be tyrannical, because it is based on externals, on what we do, and is promul-
gated through rule and regulation. Spirituality, on the other hand,
is internal, is based on what God does in and through us, and it
results from surrender. Religion has always tended to be destructive. God uses the word covenant, whereas religion has more to do
with contract. I go into a shop, I pick up a newspaper, pay the

money, and walk out the door. End of story. That was a contract. I paid the money, and the shopkeeper owed me a newspaper. When I receive the newspaper, the contract is ended, and we now owe each other nothing. A covenant, on the other hand, is something entirely different. It is an on-going openness between us, that never ends, even if one of us is unfaithful to it. I can break a contract, but not a covenant. If I work out of a contract mentality, I ask God for something, and he just has to deliver. He is obligated to me, and he must fulfil my expectations. With a covenant mentality, however, I know and believe that God has committed himself to creating me, and taking care of me every step of the way. His love is total, and it invites me to love in return. Even if I am unfaithful to him, and do not fulfil my part, the covenant is not over, and can always be renewed. In prayer, I can confidently ask God to take care of a particular issue, and leave the taking care entirely to him. If he chooses to answer my prayer through the police, the sea or air rescue service, that is his decision! All I know is that he will take care of it. God is always faithful to his covenant.

> *Holy Spirit, Breath of God! When it comes to things of God, I'm away out of my league! I know it is here that you come in, and it is for this you were sent. Please continue to reveal the Father's love to me. I want to know that love, and to be convinced and convicted of that love in my heart. That, I know, is total gift, and I look to you to obtain that gift for me. Thank you. Amen.*

21. A sign of hope

It's interesting how people 'shake down' into optimists, pessimists, moaners, groaners, and those special people who see life for the extraordinary gift that it is. All have received the same gift, but all don't see it as gift. Life is a mystery to be lived rather than a problem to be solved. I can approach life with clenched fists or with open hands. I often joke that there are people who will find something wrong in heaven, once they have had a look around! I readily admit that some people appear to get a very raw deal in life, and, as soon as they regain their standing after one disaster, they are hit by another tidal wave of trouble. I see this in parts of the world, where people are just recovering from an earthquake when they are devastated by a tropical storm. At such times, even when I don't understand, I need to remind myself that these people are part of my species, who walk on the same planet as myself, and who are also travelling on the journey of life. The question as to 'Why them, and not me?' is one of the many questions involved in the mystery of life, where the answers are being held back for now. I just have to trust and believe that there is some plan and purpose at work in all of this. I have to accept the simple fact that I cannot understand, nor need I understand the mysteries of life.

Because of what I see as a priority, I speak of attitude, more than act or action. I speak of vision, of how one perceives life to be, irrespective of what's happening in that life. Just as an Irish comedian uses the slogan 'It's the way that you tell them', so I speak of life as 'It's the way that you look at it.' I'm not sure just how much of our way of looking at life is something that we inherit, or whether our own experience of life makes us that way. It has to be some mixture of nature and nurture. Of course, I could blame my formative years for much of my negative thinking, and my less than healthy behaviour. However, I believe to do so would be dishonest. My formation can explain how I am, but it cannot continue to excuse it. I did not have control over those times, but, surely, I should be willing to take control over today.

Old habits die slowly, and a pessimistic outlook can be so ingrained that it is no longer evident to its 'owner', because it has come to be part of life's scenery. The only possible way of changing this situation is through the intervention of God, through the redemption of Jesus, and through the anointing of the Spirit. Even the ability to see how things are is, in itself, a miracle of God. Following on this is the cry for help, the 'Lord, that I may see', 'Lord, if you want to, you can heal me', 'Jesus, son of David, have pity on me.' When this cry comes from the heart it reaches the heart of God. God's reply will surely be 'What do you want me to do for you?' You then have an open line to God, and you have his full attention. Go for it! Only God, very definitely and clearly, only God can rescue you from your condition, from your blindness. When you can see again, the actual situations around you will not have changed much, but you will have changed, and everything will look completely different.

> A man had climbed out on a high bridge, and was ready to jump into the swollen river below. A policeman inched his way towards the man, trying desperately to distract him, and to hold his attention, in the hope of talking him down from his dangerous pedestal. Eventually, he got the man's attention, and he made a bargain with him. 'I'll give you two minutes to tell me what's wrong with this world, and why you want to leave it, if you give me two minutes to tell you what's right with this world, and why you should continue living in it.' The man agreed to this, and he began listing off all that is wrong with this world, and with life. He went on and on, well over the allotted time, and the policeman had great difficulty in stopping him. Now it was the turn of the policeman to list all that is good about this world, and about life. He spoke freely for over half a minute, and then he slowed down, and began to hesitate. By the time he had finished the first minute he had run out of things to say, so he just reached over, took the man by the hand, and both of them jumped!

Is it possible that we carry around within us the seeds of our own destruction? This seems to be the case with addictions and compulsions, when insane behaviour can be the norm. People who, at other times, can be quite sane, and would 'bridle' at the suggestion that they were anything other than paradigms of sanity, can be seen to act in the most insane and destructive way. The insanity is shown by repeating the same behaviour, and always hoping for a different result! There is a place of deep vulnerability within all of us, where we all have the potential to be anybody we read about in the papers, whose perversions or destructive behaviour is in the public eye. I may shudder at the thought of paedophilia, and accept that it is not part of what I experience within myself. While that is true, thank God, I just have to accept the fact that, in that inner place of vulnerability, there is the potential to be a paedophile, a sexual pervert, a mass murderer, or any other destructive personality I may read about in the paper. That should help concentrate the mind! There, but for the grace of God, go I! We are very frail, mortal, brittle creatures. Of ourselves, we just do not have the resources to disengage ourselves from the webs of our convoluted condition. Our condition is too much part of us, it is too close to us for us to be objective.We may notice some of this in others, but not easily in ourselves. This is where God, often referred to as The Higher Power, comes in. Like the policeman on the bridge, we are so limited in what we can say, and in what we can do, that we need something greater than ourselves to rescue us. It is difficult for us to accept the simple truth that we do not have, of ourselves, what it takes to succeed in the stakes of life. I suggested earlier that we might well have within us the seeds of our own destruction.

Again and again, in these reflections, I have stated that the only real sin I can commit, as a Christian, is to lose hope. This hope does not come from, or of, ourselves, no more than our faith consists in having faith in our faith. Quite often, this is nothing more than knowing a certain truth, and, therefore, is merely mental assent. Knowing that Jesus is God is not faith, because even Satan knows that. How I respond to that knowledge can be faith. We are a resurrected people, who, because of Jesus, and what he has done for us, have the victory over the three evils of sin, sickness, and death. It is because of Jesus, and of him alone, that we can have any reason for hope.

Without him, we have no reason not to jump into the nearest river! On the occasion of a funeral, for example, especially after a death that was sudden and tragic, I just cannot possibly imagine how someone, without the Christian belief, can continue to struggle with a life that has no purpose beyond the grief, and the fatality of ending in nothingness. Faith and hope are so much more than mere virtues. They form the anchors of Christian living, the foundations on which we build our lives. St Peter writes to the early Christians 'Always have an explanation to give to those who ask you the reason for the hope that you have.'

Jesus tells us that we can be the salt of the earth. Salt is a preservative that keeps things from rotting and going bad. The world of today badly needs the witness of Christian hope. There are times when one detects a sense of gloom and doom in the air. This can easily happen when bad news gets all the headlines, which is quite frequent. On the other hand, I would hate to see the day when good news would be so rare that it would merit banner headlines! I would much prefer to be helped by a light-house than a life-boat! The light-house is a preventative measure, whereas the life-boat is called in when the disaster has happened. Just as Jesus speaks of us being the salt of the earth, he also speaks of us being the light of the world. If I don't have hope in my own heart, I have nothing to offer anyone, and, here, to quote Jesus again, I become part of the blind leading the blind.

> *Lord Jesus, I think of your resurrection as the final victory over death and despair. I pray that this becomes deeply impressed in my spirit, so that I constantly live with hope, and that I always have a reason to give for the hope that I have. Lord, where there's despair in life, let me bring hope. Amen.*

22. The facts are friendly

It's a long time ago now since I first heard 'When everything else fails, try the truth; it always works'! I cannot claim to have always been faithful to that adage, but it came to haunt me whenever I failed to remember it, or to act on it. The liar has to have a good memory, because it can take several other lies to cover up the first one. I was living in the US during a particular time of political turmoil, and the cynics were telling us to hold on to our worst suspicions, because history would prove them to be correct! No one knows when the full truth is spoken, but in the intervening years it is reasonable to presume that most of the truth about those times is now out in the public arena. A lot of heart-break, and a lot of ruined careers would have been saved had the truth been spoken in the first place. This is not easy, of course, because, as a result of original sin, cover-up and denial are part of the stock-and-trade of all of us. When Adam and Eve fell for the lie in the Garden they came under new management, under the control of the Father of Lies. If they had gone up to God and confessed that they had 'blown it', I'm sure God would have said that he accepted their confession, and he would set things aright again. Unfortunately, what happened was that Adam blamed Eve, and Eve blamed the devil, and we're doing that since!

We all know quite well how the thread of deceit and lies can be woven and spun in the course of a life-time. The lies of a child are often figments of a bright imagination. They are often part of the fantasy-life of the child. However, there are lies and lies, and it is usually evident to the adult when the lies are becoming harmful to others, and particularly harmful to the person who tells them. It would be a wonderful contribution to the well-being and the formation of the young to give very particular attention in guiding them into the ways of truth at all times. As a child, I myself distinctly remember being told how important it was to tell the truth, yet I do not ever remember telling the truth, and getting rewarded for it! In fact, I have clear memories of all hell breaking loose around me when I did the right thing and told the truth!

> The young boy was doing his homework, as his dad watched television. After a while the boy raised his head from his writing to ask 'Dad, where did I come from?' The dad was taken aback, but decided to give some answer, so he replied 'The stork brought you.' The boy continued writing, and then, after a while, came another question 'And, dad, where did you come from?' The dad was more taken aback this time, but he decided to brave this one out, so he replied 'Santa Claus brought me.' There was further silence, and more writing, before yet another question 'And, dad, where did grand-dad come from?' The father was beginning to feel cornered, but he battled on bravely with 'Oh, he was found under a head of cabbage.' This was followed by a long silence, and more writing, before the copy was closed, and the boy headed up the stairs to bed. The father was wondering what had prompted all the questions. He went over, picked up the copy, opened it, and read 'As far as I can ascertain, after persistent questioning, there hasn't been a normal birth in this family for three generations'!!

Someone said one time that the essence of proper communication is the ability to combine total honesty with total kindness. I could be totally honest, while being very cruel. I could visit someone in hospital today, and, when asked 'How do you think I look?' I could reply 'You look awful, and I'll be surprised if you survive the night'! That could be the truth, and I am being totally honest, while being very very cruel. On the other hand, a parent, to keep on the good side of a child, could tell her how wonderful she is, and how proud she has made her parents, whereas, in practice, the child has been obnoxious, and really deserves some strict disciplinary action. Such a parent may think herself as being very kind, while, of course, she is being totally dishonest. When it comes to the facts of life, or, indeed, the facts of death, there are very clear guide-lines. There is seldom a need for all the truth at any one time, unless the questioner pushes for the whole truth. There is never a justification, however, for telling lies. For example, when dealing with the terminally ill, there is a golden rule: Never volunteer information, and never tell a lie. As a general rule we can take it that the person will ask when that person needs to know.

I was fed quite a lot of poppy-cock during my formative years, and I am being totally honest when I say that I don't blame anyone, because, somehow, it was part of the times. We believed in ghosts, leprechauns and banshees back then too! I was given lists and lists of sins that I have since discovered are not sins at all! I actually knew of a true incident concerning a young lad being brought to church for Confession by his older brother one Saturday morning. The younger boy was really worried because he had no sins to tell the priest, and, therefore, he was going to get into serious trouble! On the way into the church he put his finger in the holy water, and squirted some on his brother, who straightaway told him that that was a sin! The young lad was delighted to hear this. In the church he forget to take off his cap, and his brother informed him that that was another sin! Anyhow, the lad who had no sins on his way to church was delighted with the fact that, by the time he got to the confession box, he had three sins!

When I was a young lad I was aware of two reserved sins in our diocese, i.e. making poteen (illegal liquor) and going to dances during Lent. What I didn't know was that these were not sins anywhere else! I just couldn't understand how my older sisters could go a few miles down the road to a dance (another diocese), and that wasn't a sin at all! I said earlier that I don't blame anyone in particular, and yet I sometimes experience anger at the thought of all the lies I was told, as part of my religious formation. Outside the Church there was no salvation; every time I visited a church on All Souls Day there was another soul on its way from Purgatory to heaven; I had to go to Confession on Saturday if I wished to receive Communion on Sunday, etc., etc. As life goes on, and I begin to see one myth after another being exploded, I could easily end up wondering if any of it is true! To be totally honest, during all the recent and not so recent scandals in the Church, I had a certain sense that all of this will only come out right when everyone is ready to speak the truth, and not retreat to denial and lies. Because I believe that the Spirit of God is renewing the Church, then I shouldn't be surprised if all dimensions of the Church, the personnel, the structure, the finances, the teachings, etc., etc., should be exposed to the spotlight of truth, so that anything unbecoming should be seen for what it is, and be removed from where it never belonged. 'When everything else fails, try the truth, because it always works'! The facts are always friendly …

Heavenly Father, I thank you for the sure, direct, simple, and personal way in which you have revealed yourself to us. Jesus never said anything unless you told him to. I depend on your Spirit, of course, to reveal the full meaning of that message. All I can do is continue to declare my willingness to listen, and my readiness to obey. By myself, I can never depend on actually doing any of that, so I trust you to avail of my good-will. Amen.

23. Forgiving and forgetting

It has been said that when God forgives, he suffers from total amnesia, and he completely forgets! If I approach him to admit 'Lord, I did that again', he could well ask 'Again?', because he has forgotten what happened on a previous occasion. It is also said that when God forgives sins he dumps them in the deepest lake. The problem for us is that he puts a sign on the lake which says 'No fishing'. There can be a tendency on our part to rake over the old coals again and again, because we find it difficult to deal with such unusual and unconditional love. Real faith is the courage to totally accept God's acceptance of us. God created us in his image and likeness, but, unfortunately, we often return the compliment! It can be so difficult for us to accept someone who is so different from us, or who insists on doing things in a way with which we are unfamiliar. I don't think it is possible for us to understand just how 'blinkered' we are in our attempts to get some understanding of God. We will never understand God, of course, not even in heaven, but, through the work of his Spirit, we can actually come to experience something of what God really is. In the words of St Paul, we can develop the mind and heart of Christ.

Jesus in the gospel was Saviour. He was not Lord yet, because he did not yet have the victory, and he could not yet give the Holy Spirit. When his victory over sin, sickness, and death was completed, he then could return to the Father in triumph, be given the kingdom, and send the Spirit to complete his work on earth. My first encounter with Jesus has to be as Saviour, because my own sinfulness is my only point of departure. Repenting, turning towards Jesus, needs to be as constant and as regular for my spiritual wellbeing, as breathing is for my physical existence. The only 'yes' God is interested in is my last one, and I cannot live today on the good intentions, or on the graces of yesterday. Once Jesus has been accepted and established as Saviour, the process of salvation has begun. I cannot give myself totally to God in any one effort. I come to the Lord like a vast tract of uncultivated land, and he redeems me bit by bit, piece by piece, area by area. Today he is reminding me of decisions that need be made in the area of speech, tomorrow in the area of time or money, and the next day it may have to do with abuse of some of his gifts. The process in on-going, and, to be successful, it must continually be making inroads into my tendency to deny or to cover up. It must lead towards greater honesty and integrity, because that is the work of the Spirit, who leads out of the darkness of deceit and lies, and into the kingdom of light and truth. Only there and only then will I be free.

It was a few summers ago. For the first time ever, the Irish international soccer team were becoming a force to be reckoned with in the European championships. I used celebrate Eucharist in a cancer ward of a Dublin city hospice. There was one man there, Hugh, who fascinated me. He was a totally committed soccer supporter, and he watched every single game, day after day. Not only that, but his sons brought in videos of matches recorded from other channels than the one he watched, so that he could watch the same game all over again, with different commentators! This was at the beginning of the summer, and those early weeks went quickly by, as game followed game.

My own work brought me elsewhere for the next few weeks, and by the time I returned to that ward the European championships were merely a memory. Hugh was still alive, but was very weak. No longer could he sit up, unaided, or have the energy to get very enthusiastic about anything. Day after day I stopped by, and we chatted some. Gradually, the conversation became more serious, as Hugh began speaking of dying, his questions, and his fears about death, and how he felt right there, right then. One day, in response to a question, I attempted to help him understand what death might be like. I spoke of the television, the videos, the replays. I spoke of the big screens available in many of the larger pubs, where the patrons gathered for every game, and it was as near to being actually present as was possible.

I suggested that this might be what happens when I die: Jesus puts me sitting down in front of a big screen, and he turns on a video called 'This is Your Life'. At the beginning, I am quite anxious and nervous, because I'm certainly not too sure just what's going to appear on the screen! As the video continues, I become aware of something rather unusual. There are blanks, which become more and more frequent as the story unfolds. There are short blanks, and some rather long ones. This continues to puzzle me, and, finally, I ask the reason for this. The answer amazes me. These were times when I did something wrong, which I admitted, and I asked Jesus to take care of it. And what do you think Jesus did? He just pressed the erase button, and the incident was wiped clean. Even now, if I asked him, he would not remember, because that is how Jesus forgives.

The outcome of the story for both Hugh and myself, was to be grateful that, when we die, we will judged by God, rather than by people!

Love, by definition, is something that calls for reciprocation, for a response. Most of us know of a mother, for example, who is heartbroken, because, despite her best efforts, a son or a daughter seems bent on self-destruction, through alcohol or some other drug. Her love is real, even intense, but there is no way that the other is even remotely capable of returning that love in kind. More than likely, by now, the son or daughter probably is filled with self-loathing, and, therefore, not capable of loving anyone, or anything. (It may surprise some of us to learn that the alcoholic, while compelled to feed a tyrannical addiction, may actually hate alcohol, because of a personal awareness of the destruction being effected, and a sense of powerlessness to do anything about it.) There is no way that I can meet God's love on anything like an equal basis. This is neither required, nor is it possible. All that is required from me is that I continue to be open to God's love, even when I cannot love myself. God loves me because he is good, not because I am good, or I deserve his love.

Forgiveness is an essential ingredient in love. If a couple knelt in front of me to get married, and they had neither a lot of money nor a lot of sense, I would proceed with the ceremony if I felt they had enough forgiveness in their hearts. Forgiveness is what will keep their love alive. When I was a child we used kill a pig every year, and the cut-up pieces were placed in tea-chests, and packed tight with salt. This was before we had freezers, and it was the salt that kept the bacon from going bad. I think of forgiveness as the salt that keeps love healthy and life-giving. Because God is love, it is reasonable to expect that forgiveness should have a very high priority with God in his dealings with us. God knows us through and through, he knows what we're made of. Have you ever noticed yourself, with the most loving heart, getting momentarily annoyed at the young or the elderly when they do or say something stupid? We tend to forget, don't we? God doesn't forget our human condition, and the ways in which we are damaged by original sin. He is more than willing to forget, however, those moments and acts of selfishness, once we are willing to accept and confess them as such. In fact, like any loving parent, he must rejoice to see that we are learning, and, when we are wrong, we begin to promptly admit it. That must gladden his heart, because it sure is a very clear sign of growth towards wholesomeness and holiness. God never has a problem with truth....

Lord Jesus, I thank you for the whole wonderful package of forgiveness, salvation, and redemption. I take all my sins and throw them into the sea of your infinite mercy. Lord, where else could I go, to whom else could I go? Without you, I would be in total despair. With you I can hope, trust, and believe that all will be well. With all my heart, I accept you as my Saviour. Thank you, Lord. Amen.

24. Letting the light shine through

I would much rather be guided safely by a light-house, than be rescued by a life-boat! I meet people who are in the rescue and recovery business, after the disaster happens. Their service is vital, and very necessary. There are others who, by their advice, example, or concern are in the business of preventing the disaster happening. It is interesting to note a shift of emphasis in recent years from traditional medicine towards preventative medicine. This would be just wonderful, of course, if this trend continued. Not that I have any problem with traditional medicine. Far from it. What I'm referring to here is best seen by comparing the drive to reduce the number of smokers in our society, and the money and time being spent treating smoking-related cancer. I readily admit, of course, that all of this is more a question of education than persuasion. If a person doesn't want to do something, then all the scare tactics in the world will make no impression whatever.

The most I can be for another person is a sign-post. Sign-posts point the way, but they certainly don't compel anybody to travel that way! Witnessing is at the centre of Christianity. I am called to be a sign, and, indeed, quite often a sign of contradiction. What I live may be a total contradiction to the ways and the wisdom of the world. As Christians, we have a charter for living, a blue-print for peace, a road map for guidance. It is about the attitudes we can develop if we wish to change things. In Matthew's gospel, chapter 5, these are called The Beatitudes. Without ever getting into a pulpit or up on a butter-box, I may be preaching values that are totally opposite to those held by the world around me. What I am is my message, rather than anything I say. If I go into your house and tell you I have measles, while I actually have chicken-pox, which are you most likely to pick up?! 'What you are doing speaks so loudly

that I just cannot hear what you're saying'! Jesus was a sign of contradiction, and this proved too much for some of the religious leaders, and so they decided to silence him, rather than listen to him. At
the beginning, Jesus said that he was the light of the world, and,
before he left, he told his followers that they were to be such a light
from then on. They should let this light shine, so that people would
see just what God was doing in them, for them, and through them.
It is said that the greatest witness an alcoholic can give is to walk,
sober, down the main street of his own town! Mary's Magnificat is
about the great things God is doing in her. I could say this sentence
in two different ways, and give two totally different meanings:
'Look what wonderful things the Lord has done for ME' or 'Look
what wonderful things the LORD has done for me.' Jesus told the
apostles that they would receive power from on high, and then they
would be his witnesses to the ends of the earth. In other words, with
the privilege would come the responsibility. 'Freely, freely, you
have received. Freely, freely give ...'.

The young mother and her four-year-old son were down town
shopping. The mother called into a church to say a few prayers.
She was moving from shrine to shrine lighting a few candles,
while Junior was having a ball, running around, and examining
everything. He pointed to a statue and asked 'Who's that?'
'That's Holy God', his mother told him. Another statue, another
question, and the answer: 'That's Holy God's mother'. The
mother had finished her prayers, and was about to leave, when
she realised that the young lad was not with her. She called his
name, got no reply, and, before she got too anxious, she located
him. He was up in the sanctuary, and he was totally fascinated
by what he had discovered. The sun was shining brilliantly
through the stained-glass windows, and, as he stood there with
his arms out sideways, he was enthralled by the many colours
on his hands, his arms, his clothes. He pointed to the stained-
glass windows and asked 'Mammy, who are those?' 'Those are
the saints', his mother told him.

Some days later, he was at play-school. The teacher happened to
mention something about saints, and the young lad got all excited.
'Miss, Miss,' he shouted. 'I know who they are.' 'What do you
mean? What are you talking about?' 'The saints. I know who

they are.' 'Well,' said the teacher, 'who are the saints?' 'The saints are the people who let the light shine through', came the very definite answer.

St John's gospel begins on a very poetic note, and it uses strong powerful images. It speaks of life and death, of good and evil, of light and darkness. It sets out clearly the opposing forces in the eternal struggle, and proceeds to show how Jesus has come to bring that struggle to its final end. Jesus is the Light that has come into a world of darkness. It is a light that is literally the eternal flame, and that will continue, so that his followers need never be in the dark again. Once there was a dark cave down in the depths of the earth, and it had never seen light. One day the sun invited it to come up to visit it. When the cave saw the light of the sun, it was totally mesmerised, and it invited the sun to come down to visit it the following day, because the sun had never seen darkness. The following day the sun came down, entered the cave, looked around, and asked: 'Where's the darkness?'! Once Jesus enters the darkness of our cave there can never be darkness there again.

Our vocation is to let that light shine on those around us. We can do that with nothing more sophisticated than a smile, or a warm handshake. Everything I do or say is inspired by what is within. This is something I cannot fake, even if I pretend for a while. We all experience our own share of dark moments, but, perhaps, it is so much easier for us to see and understand darkness in the lives of others. Some people's facial expressions betoken the darkness within. Quite a lot of money is spent in an attempt to dispel that darkness, through counselling, group work, or medication. All of this has its place, and I wouldn't belittle any of it. However, all human endeavour is beset with the mortality and limitations of humanity. In other words, the solution will not last. Only Jesus is the same yesterday, today, and always.

In our own age, as in all previous ages, the Lord provides significant role models for all of us, so that we can see in them exactly what is meant by a human person being 'a light to the nations,... and to those who sit in darkness, and in the shadow of death.' Yes, of course, the saints are the people who let the light shine through. We limit all hope of understanding saints, of course, if we confine our definition of saints to those who are dead, and to those who are canonised. Everyone of us must know real-life, flesh and blood, living saints in our everyday lives. They don't ever have to be canonised, and they don't have to die to become 'Holy Souls'! They are holy souls now, they are probably fully human and fully alive, and they certainly give life and light to those around them. I thank God for all the saints I know and have known. They make it easier for me to believe in Jesus and in his message, whenever I come across someone in whom it is all seen to work.

Holy Spirit, Spirit and Breath of God, I open my heart to the light of Christ which you have come to light in my heart. I trust you to work away within my heart, day after day, so that, thanks to you, and to your work, that inner light may shine on those I meet. I don't want to be a source of that light, or to be seen as the source. I just ask that I might bring light to those who sit in darkness, and in the shadow of death. Amen.

25. A fountain in the heart

Beneath the driest desert there is water aplenty, but it is just not accessible. I know very little about geology or earth structure, but it wouldn't surprise me to hear that the centre of the earth is made up of some sort of liquid. We deal with this concept on a regular basis, whether I squeeze an orange, or shake a raw egg. The other surface tends to be protective, and therefore more solid, for an inner core that needs protection. The inner core generally contains the source of life, the seed, the embryo. As a Christian, I believe the words of Jesus about a spring of living water within the heart of all his followers. This is not actually water, of course, but is very highly significant. It is a source of life, refreshment, invigoration. God's Spirit is spoken of as having being breathed into the form of clay, so that the first person became alive. We speak of life here, whether we use the symbols of water, light, fire, wind, or breath. I particularly like the image of water, because of the many significant uses it has. It speaks of cleansing, of refreshing, of slaking thirst. Someone on hunger strike could go for many days without food, but not for very long without water. In fact, when food is withdrawn, the intake of water must be significantly increased.

It is interesting to notice the words we use that have water connotations. When a speaker is dull and uninspiring, he is said to be very dry! Humour that is not bubbly and infectious is spoken of as a dry humour. When there is a plentiful supply of anything, from replies to an advertisement, to letters of condolences, the messages are said to be flooding in. The lands of famine are parched, and the football stadium is awash with emotion, expectation, and excitement. I recently had some regular contact with a friend who mounted an art exhibition, based on the theme of water. There was the source of a river, a waterfall, still pools, fast-running shallow waters, etc. I was asked to write some general reflections on the exhibition, for inclusion in the programme. I found great inspiration in the exercise, because every picture was an aspect of some kind of life, and all of it was engaged in moving ever onwards towards a final destination in a sea or ocean. While each aspect reflected a different reality, they all shared a common destiny.

A very devout and good priest had served for many years in a big downtown parish, and he decided to shift gears in middle-age by moving to the parish of a small rural congregation. This happened many years ago, but this is the way he still tells the story of his first big country meal in the house of one of the parishioners. 'The eating was good, it was almost sinful: baked ham, fried chicken, and roast beef; sweet potatoes, mashed potatoes, and vegetable casseroles dripping with butter; fresh-baked bread and rolls, and, for desert, hot blueberry pie, topped with huge wedges of home-made vanilla ice-cream. All through that sumptuous meal, there was something bothering and distracting me, and it adversely effected my enjoyment of the meal. All during the dinner I could hear the sound of running water, and it really bothered me. Back in the city, that sound was bad news. Someone had left a tap running, and the sink or tub was about to overflow, or there was a leak in the plumbing, and the ceiling was about to cave in. For two hours I listened to, and heard little else but the sound of running water. However, since it was my first visit to this parishioner's house, I was reluctant to say anything, hoping against hope that one of my genial hosts would begin hearing what I was hearing. Finally, I could no longer contain my inner frustration, so I mentioned it, and asked about it. With a smile, my host explained the situation to me. It seems that forty years before, when the people had built the farmhouse, they discovered a spring of water right in the centre of the property. They built a spring room around it, and then planned and built the rest of the house around that inner spring room. For forty years, the people who lived in that house had come to be fully conscious of that spring of water right at the very core of their home, and its significance for them grew with the years. I thought to myself, "That is what Jesus is constantly trying to tell us: that it is possible to build the rooms of our lives around the life-giving spring of God's Spirit".'

What a wonderful idea! Each of us has the potential to do this, even in the most crowded living conditions. The Spirit is total gift. When the Spirit came upon Mary, Life itself began to form within her. This is life-giving at its most profound, and is available to all of us, 'to you, and to all your children', as Peter said on the morning of Pentecost. There is a wonderful story in the book of Ezekiel (chapter 37), which is one of the books in the Old Testament. The prophet was brought down into a valley full of dry bones that were scattered everywhere on the ground. He was told that the bones represented God's people, who had lost hope, and who no longer had a zest for life and living. The image is both powerful and significant. I needn't go into any great detail about the story here, except that God brought the bones together, put flesh and skin on them, and so had a large army of lifeless bodies. It was then that he called on the Spirit to enter the bodies, and they came alive, and became like an army on the march. This was God's way of showing his people how he intended to revive them. As dry bones, they symbolised a people bereft of life, and of God's Spirit. They represented sheer emptiness, the very opposite to people who have a fountain of living water within.

Getting in touch with this inner fountain of life can be a source of inspiration during prayer. This fountain rises up from within, as Jesus says. It can bring many things to the surface, for forgiveness, for healing, or even for accepting. During prayer, I can reflect on what is going on deep within my spirit, and thus, as with all life-giving prayer, be conscious of what is happening, rather than anything I myself am doing. In the words of Scripture, and, indeed, in the direct personal words of Jesus, I get in touch with my deep inner thirst. 'If anyone is thirsty, let that person come to me ...' says Jesus. 'Come to the water, all you who are thirsty, ... receive freely, without money ....' Earlier in this reflection, I spoke of water as a source of life. Jesus said that he came so we would have life, and have that life in abundance. Life in abundance! What a wonderful concept, especially when we think of those times when we settle for existing, dragging our feet from one day to the next, without any sense of privilege or excitement. 'He died at thirty, and was buried at eighty' would be a sad comment on a life, and the person in question!

It is said that there is no such thing as a real atheist. I'm not sure about that, but I'm inclined to believe that. It is said that there are no atheists in fox-holes, or in rubber dinghies out in the middle of the Atlantic! Was it George Bernard Shaw who said 'I am an atheist, thank God!'? There is a conscious thirst within, and it must be very difficult indeed, if not impossible, to live a life and succeed in ignoring that. There are many other ways, of course, in which people try to quench that inner thirst, and the scrap-heaps of humanity are piled up with the wreckage that results from such futility ... With his dying breath, Jesus said 'I thirst ...'

Spirit and Breath of God, thinking of you as a fountain of living water within me, is one of the greatest consolations of my life. I often feel so arid, so dry, and then I remember that, beneath the driest desert, there is plenty of water. Please fill and refresh my whole being, and bring me into a whole new growth. I trust you to prevent me getting shrivelled, insipid, and lifeless. Please ensure that I am open to life in abundance. Amen.

26. When the going gets tough

Most of us are cradle-Catholics, or, at least, cradle-Christians. We were brought to church for Baptism, and we ourselves were never involved in that decision in any way. Later on, before we reached a level of maturity whereby we could be involved in a free personal decision, we were brought to church again, this time for Confirmation. This meant that a bishop was brought along to confirm what had happened at our Baptism. There are many and varied arguments about delaying the second of those trips until the individual concerned is in a position to make some kind of mature, life-long commitment. When I was growing up, I belonged to a Church which dealt in numbers, where there was a universal acceptance of procedures, that had little to do with individual input. We all marched to the beat of the one drum, and dissent was neither expected nor accepted. There was a social dimension to religion, where the norm was to do what everybody else was doing, irrespective of personal misgivings or opinions.

I now believe that we are moving towards a more healthy and more vibrant church. It will be much smaller by way of numbers, but the quality of the commitment will be much better. I see us moving towards a church that will be made up of smaller numbers, but much more committed people. Many good bishops travelled to the sessions of Vatican II, convinced that the church was in good shape. This came from the tendency to head-count, where the numbers attending church gatherings was taken as a sign of health. After all, practising Catholics were those who went to Mass on Sundays, without any great expectations for the rest of the week! History, and what has happened since the Council, seem to show that God may not have had the same eye-view of how things were. It will be seen, in time, as the end of an era, and the beginning of something new. Pope John XXIII prayed for a whole new Pentecost, and it would seem that his prayer was answered. Change is always difficult in a large and ancient institution, where there had been very little change in over a century.

It is easy for an institution like the church to see itself in the business of changing the world in which it is, and forget that the church itself also has to be open to change. For many decades prior to this time, the spirituality was a Jesuit spirituality, reduced to a simple theme of seeing God in all things. The documents of the Council gave new perspectives on spirituality. Firstly, it had to be relevant and realistic, and, therefore, always open to change. Relevance is an important word here. Most young people I know are not actually against the church. It is simply that they do not see the church as having any relevance for them. It just does not belong to the world in which they live. Secondly, there is a personal dimension to spirituality, that had been forgotten for many decades. Humans have reason, will, and feelings, and a spirituality that does not allow for these vital ingredients, is bound to by-pass the very people it is meant to serve. Thirdly, there is a social or communitarian aspect to spirituality, and we are heading into cul-de-sacs when the emphasis is on God and us, without equal reference to our interaction with each other. Lastly, spirituality must be humble enough, and realistic enough, to avail of the insights of the social sciences, especially psychology. For example, candidates for priesthood, and the Religious Life, can benefit enormously from personality profiles, aptitude tests, counselling, etc. All of this calls for a much deeper level of activity, and not some superficial skimming of the surface, when the structures are no longer there to support and maintain such a spirituality.

There was a group of Christians gathered in prayer in Russia, before the fall of communism was even considered. Suddenly the door was broken down by the boot of a soldier, who entered with a sub-machine gun. He looked around the room, paused for a few seconds, and then quietly announced 'O.K., any of you folks who don't really believe in Jesus, get out now, while you have a chance.' There was a short, silent pause, and then, one by one, people began to make their way to the exit. Very soon most of them had left. A small group remained. They had thought this through, they foresaw such a possibility, and they had long since made their decision about what to do in such an event. The soldier looked around at them for a while. He then proceeded to close the door, and to return to face the group. They didn't know what to expect. Imagine their surprise, therefore, when the soldier smiled, and said 'Actually, I believe in Jesus too, and I believe we're much better off without those'!

In John's gospel, chapter six, Jesus was faced with a dilemma. Many of his followers took exception to what he was saying. They said 'This is a hard saying, and who can take it?' Scripture then tells 'they turned and left, and walked no more with him.' It is interesting to note that Jesus didn't run after them, and try to reason with them. He didn't withdraw anything of what he said, and he didn't try to convince them that it wasn't all that bad. No, they had made a decision, and he let them go. As a matter of fact, he turned to those who remained, and proceeded to challenge them! 'Will you also go away?' In other words, please feel free to do so, if you wish. Someone said one time that there are three groups of people in any gathering: A small group who cause things to happen; a larger group who watch things happening; and the vast majority who haven't a clue what's happening!

Again and again, in these reflections, I am saying that God doesn't send me anywhere when I die. Rather will he eternalise whatever decision I make now. 'You are either for me or against me. They that are not with me, are against me.' In my younger (and more naïve?) days, I had great admiration for those people who died as martyrs. I considered them extremely brave, single-minded, and totally committed. In essence, I would still hold this to be true, except that I would insert one very significant factor. The ability to stick to their Christian commitment, no matter what, is something that I now see as total gift. In other words, the greatest coward can become a martyr, if she/he is open to the graces that come from being a committed Christian. It would make no sense, of course, to think that I could be totally committed to the Lord, without the sure and certain expectation that the Lord would be totally committed to me. God is never out-done in generosity. Any level of commitment on my part comes directly from my conviction of his commitment to me. Anything that comes from me is a direct response to what I perceive as coming to me. To have any hope of ever understanding this, I must always be willing to begin with the Lord. If I begin with myself, I head into serious trouble. Firstly, I'm turning the divine initiative into human endeavour, and, secondly, to begin with myself is a sure way to end up in despair. Even after all these years, original sin can still slip in, and claim eventual success! The Christian vocation is a package. With the call comes what it takes to answer and live the call. That is why Christianity has always witnessed to extraordinary levels of commitment down the years. There is one central point, however, that must be stressed again and again. So that God's power can clearly be seen as the inspiration and the driving force, God tends to choose very weak people to do his greatest work!

Lord Jesus, I do want to belong to you. I want you to have full access to all that I am. I open my heart, all of my inner being, and I invite you, Lord, to take over there completely. I ask your Spirit to melt every speck of coldness and lukewarmness, to stir up within me a zeal and enthusiasm for things of God, and to enkindle within me the fires of divine love. Amen.

27. He just didn't do anything

Whatever we say about Christianity being an inspiration, being personal Incarnation, being an invitation to share in the life of the Trinity, we must not overlook the fact that, basically, it is about action. Jesus gives us a preview of the General Judgement in Matthew's gospel (chapter 25). There are no questions about visions, ecstasies, or any kind of religious, spiritual, or mystic experiences. The questions are scandalously materialistic. I will be asked about a slice of bread, a cup of water, an article of clothing. 'What did you do? What did you do?' will be the questions ringing in my ears, as each scene of my life is relayed before me. Jesus takes all this doing very personally, because he identifies so strongly with the weak, the marginalised, the outcast, that he takes what I do for them as being done for him. He also knows only too well, of course, that the road to hell is paved with good intentions, and, when all is said and done, there's much more said than done! He tells us that 'not all who call me Lord will enter the kingdom of heaven; only those who do the will of my Father in heaven.' Again and again, Jesus returns to this theme. 'These people honour me with their lips ...'

The Christian symbol is the cross. This is made up of an horizontal and a vertical beam. The horizontal beam represents God and me, while the vertical beam represents me and others. There must be a balance between these two. God doesn't want to hear me tell him that I'm sorry, I'm thankful, or I praise him, unless the people on either side of me hear it also. What comes down from God to me, e.g., forgiveness, must go sideways to others; otherwise it stops coming from God. In plain and simple words, Jesus said if we want to receive mercy, compassion, or forgiveness from God, then let us begin by giving all of that to others. For someone who is not a Christian, this must seem very simple, patently obvious, and deeply puzzling. Deeply puzzling, because history has shown many Christians to have anything but the characteristics of Christ. Mahatma Ghandi, while working in London during his early life, was given a copy of the gospels to read. His verdict: Having read the gospels, I have come to admire your Christ, and to despise your Christianity. When I say that a non-Christian must see our mandate as very simple, I mean that nothing could be more direct and less complicated than to be told 'As you would that others should do to you, do you also to them in like manner. For the measure with which you give is the measure that will be used to give to you.'

Albert Camus, in his novel called 'The Fall', gives a very graphic account of a situation in which one man found himself. It was late at night, and he was in a red-light district of Amsterdam. Close by, he heard a woman scream, and he was fairly certain that, at that moment, she had been thrown into the canal. His first instinct was to rush to her rescue. Caution and prudence, however, took over, and he remained where he was. What if the person, or persons, who threw her in were still in the area? His own life would be at risk. What if the police came along? A press photographer? Would his name, and even his picture make it to the front pages of the newspaper? How was he, a legal eagle of some stature and renown, going to explain his presence in such a part of town, at such a late hour? The arguments within, were flying fast and furious. By that stage, the cries of the woman had died down, and were no longer audible. By now it was probably too late, anyhow. There was nothing he could do at this stage.

Camus concludes his description of the incident with these chilling words: He didn't do anything, because that was the kind of man he was.

I remember those words searing my soul the first time I read them. They jumped at me from the page. At that time, I considered the comment among the worst possible things that could be said about anybody. Again and again in these reflections, I stress that life is not about achieving anything, or arriving at some goal. It is about effort, good-will, doing something, having a go. It is about us being good soil for God's word, even if we only produce thirty percent. It is termed good soil, because it produced something. God is not a tyrant, who demands the impossible. He is full of compassion and understanding. He gives us the wonderful gift of life to be used in the service of others, and it must surely upset him when this gift is not used. The upset comes from several reasons. Firstly, he gives us nothing for ourselves, and a life that is not spent in the service of others is a life that is wasted. Secondly, it is only by giving to others that we ourselves receive anything, and God really feels sorry for us when we deprive ourselves of all the love and the life that he wants us to have. 'He didn't do anything, because that was the kind of man he was', speaks of someone who is alienated from God, and from others, and who lives permanently in solitary confinement, with nobody else in his life but himself. That is certainly not God's plan and purpose for us.

Imagine I gathered a group of people in a room. I then proceeded to take apart every single component in the engine of a car. I hand a part of the engine to everybody in the room, and, for the sake of our example, the numbers tally between the parts and the people. I then invite the people to reflect on the various roles we are called to play, as we live out our Christian vocation. Each one of us has a specific function that cannot be done by anyone else. If I accept my place, and make available that which is entrusted to me, then the engine will work. In Christian terms we speak of each of us being a member in the Body of Christ. Each member has a function that is unique, and yet it is something on which the other members depend. Christianity calls me to be accountable for the gifts God has given me.

There is an extraordinary dualism in Christianity. On the one hand, I pray as if all depends on God, while on the other, I work as if all depends on me. I just cannot sit back, and expect God to do everything, like the man whose beard went on fire, and he prayed that it might rain! On the other hand, I take on the activity with the simple principle: Unless the Lord build the house, in vain do the builders labour. I sow the seed, and I trust the Lord to provide the increase. I deliberately sound a note of caution here, because there is a happy medium between inactivity and the heresy of good works. The combination and balance between the vertical and horizontal of the cross is the ideal. I go to God (in prayer) for the sake of others, and I go to others (work) for the sake of God. I must never get so involved in the work of the Lord that I end up neglecting the Lord of the work. As in so many aspects of life, it is about striking a proper and healthy balance.

'What you do speaks so loudly that I cannot hear what you are saying' can be a statement of commendation or condemnation. My actions can be of such witness value that I don't need to open my mouth to be a preacher of the gospel. 'You write a new page of the gospel each day, by the things that you do, and the words that you say. People read what you write, whether faithful and true. What is the gospel according to you?' Before being asked to preach, or teach the gospel, I am firstly asked to live it ...

Holy Spirit, Spirit of God, I have to trust you totally to please continue to urge me into action. I know rightly just how I can drift, and become aimless. Please continue to challenge me, to remind me, to enthuse me. Without you, I would very quickly run out of steam, and settle for existing. I open my heart to the full possibility of life in abundance. Amen.

28. Make-up-your-mind time

There is a vast difference between religion and spirituality. Religion is external, made up of rules, regulations, and procedures, and it is about control. Most religious people spend their lives trying to please God, and, at the end of the day, they're not too sure they have succeeded. Unfortunately, the efforts to please God are usually based on rules and commandments. 'If I do this, that, and the other, God will be pleased with me.' We see God as a demanding God, and we are here to meet his every whim. We get into the numbers game, as we multiply prayers, and we are often trying to beat the clock, to ensure that we 'get in' the prayers. Prayers become more powerful according to the number of times we say them, and numbers like nine (Novena) have been given a leverage that borders on the superstitious. Religious people have their eyes set on getting to heaven, and life is one long battle to accumulate enough points to qualify. Even at the end of all that, not many religious people will tell you that they are sure of getting to heaven. Religious people are good people. Jesus, however, could do nothing with religious people, and they ended up killing him. He wanted them to change, and when you are fixed and rooted in definitives, how can you possibly consider changing? To do so is paramount to admitting that we might have been wrong up till then. Religious people cannot afford to be wrong, because they consider that there is only one way to do things, and they have found it.

Spirituality, on the other hand, is internal, it is what God does in us, and it is about surrender. Rather than religion, which is based on a love of law, spirituality is based on a law of love. It involves Incarnation, where God's Spirit makes it possible for Jesus to become flesh in us, to make his home in us, and to take on everything we are. For spirituality to grow and to become more and more powerful in us, we must be prepared to get out of the way, and let God be God. God becomes God in my life, the very moment I stop playing God. Spirituality is based on the 'Yes ... be it done onto me according to your word' of Mary. This is the door that opens our hearts to the action of God's Spirit. There is no place for muscular Christianity, where we become members of the 'white knuckle club.' God's work in us is total gift, and it is only through what Jesus has done, and what the Spirit continues to do in us that we can become other Christ's, members of his body, children of the Father.

It is very easy for any of us to slip into the trap of doing the right things for the wrong reasons. As I said, religious people are, essentially, good people. I don't, for one moment, think that God would punish them for not doing things his way, because, in general, I would fully accept that most of them act out of sincere good-will, and noble intentions. Pure religion, however, has a great deal of the components of original sin about it, and this could never be claimed as being of God. I sometimes think of religious people as those who are only half redeemed, and they themselves are completing the programme! God always loves the sinner, even if he detests the sin. I often think that Satan never feels very threatened by religion! In fact, some of the religion I have witnessed over the years had some of his distinctive marks on it. Millions of people have been killed down the centuries, and all done in God's name. There are very few wars in today's world that are not religious wars. Religion has often been seen as destructive, and, accepting that God is love, it is doubtful if any of that had anything to do with God. The nearest I'll ever come to actually seeing God on this earth is if I ever come across two people who really love one another. 'By this shall all people know that you are my disciples, if you have love, one for another.'

There was a fancy-dress ball in the town. It was a very important part of the social life of the area, and people went to great lengths to come up with something new and original each year. This year one man dressed up as Satan, and, at the instigation of his friends, he decided to walk down the main street in full costume, on his way to the ball. Unfortunately, for him, the heavens (?!) opened, and the rain came pouring down. He ran for shelter. There was a door open, and it was the door of the parish hall, so in he went. What he hadn't known was that there was a prayer meeting in progress. Imagine the shock for the people gathered there, when 'Satan' ran in the door! They scattered in all directions! There was a second door at the other end of the hall, and they dashed for that exit. One old lady caught her coat in the corner of a bench, and she felt trapped. As 'Satan' approached, she panicked, and felt that there was no escape for her. In desperation, she cried out 'Satan, I know I have gone to Mass every morning for the past forty years, but, I want you to know, honestly, that, during all that time, I was really on your side'!

Jesus said 'You are either for me, or against me. They who do not gather with me, scatter.' The only advantage Satan has is numbers. On his side are those who are overtly involved in evil, as well as those who haven't made any decision, one way or another. In the last book of the Bible (Revelations), God says 'I wish that you were either hot or cold! But because you are lukewarm, I will begin to vomit you out of my mouth.' To use our own language for something that provokes that reaction in us: 'You make me sick!' And those are the words of an all-loving God! Jesus has the utmost love and compassion for the broken, the outcast, and the marginalised, but he poured his wrath and scorn on the religious leaders who thought themselves above what he had to offer. 'You say that all is well with you, because you have Abraham for your father. God could raise up someone like Abraham from those very stones!'

During my years of teaching religious knowledge in schools, I frequently came across the pupil who was all set for a discussion. Now discussion has its place, of course, and it is important that people are allowed express their point of view, and that they listen to the points of view of others. One of the ways, however, of never getting around to doing anything is to discuss it long enough! The word that became flesh can be turned back into word again, if the discussion process is prolonged. I believe that Jesus is much more interested in decision than in discussion. I know it's a cliché, but how true it is: All that is needed for evil people to succeed is that good people do nothing. The woman in our story could have drifted from day to day, without any great personal input, and be like the bishop who dreamt he was preaching a sermon, and when he woke up, he was!

The whole purpose of these reflections is to get people to think.

Again and again, I have said that a life without reflection is not worth living. Alice in Wonderland begins her story with the words: 'I could tell you my story, beginning this morning. I couldn't begin yesterday, because I was a different person then.' Cardinal Suenens says 'My God is new with each new day.' Satan must dearly love to lull us into a sense of security, so that, like the apostles in Gethsemane, we doze off asleep. Jesus calls us to 'Watch, and pray', to be alert, to be present to the moment. Jesus of Nazareth is passing by. Each moment is gift, every problem is an opportunity, and every day is a whole new life in miniature. For the person who is open to the gift of life, and to the surprises of each new day, then Satan must surely know that such a person was never on his side!

Lord Jesus, with all my heart, I declare that I want to belong totally to you. I want to be totally available to you, to your work, and to your kingdom. I can never trust myself in this, so I depend on your Spirit of truth to ensure that I am being genuine, authentic, and sincere. With each day I offer you all that I am, whatever good-will I have, whatever time is mine. I have to trust the rest to you. Thanks, Lord. Amen.

29. The measure with which you give

There is a saying about computers: Feed in junk, and you'll get out junk. The same is true about life. You get back what you invest. If you are a life-giver to others, you will receive life from them. There is a book called 'The Happiest People on Earth', and it was written by the founder of the Full Gospel Fellowship International. He is speaking, of course, of those people who are in the business of being concerned for the welfare of others. Those whose lives revolve around themselves are most to be pitied, because this brings a profound sense of isolation and loneliness. 'It is not good for man/woman to be alone.' No man/woman is an island, we each belong to the mainland, and Mother Teresa tells us that the greatest hunger on earth is not for food, but for a sense of belonging, for a sense of being loved. On a flippant, superficial level, one could think that God was being particularly clever in all this. He arranged things in such a way that we were put in control of what we get back from life. It is a kind of 'over to you' situation, and we do have a great say in whatever sense of worth our lives may have.

On a personal note, I was blessed in being brought up in a family where both my parents did everything within their power to give us whatever they had to give. It was not a perfect family, because there is no such thing! We were a 'good-enough' family, which seems to rate fairly high on the national average! To be honest with you, I certainly would not like to grow up in a perfect family (being that there's no such thing!), because I would not at all be prepared to face the realities that life has thrown at me over the years! I imagine I would have become a veritable duckling in a world of swans, an innocent abroad, a dreamer in a world of reality. I mention my family for the simple reason that I lived to see both my parents getting back, more than a hundred-fold, everything they had put into rearing us. It is part of Muslim teaching that, when I am caring for my parents, I, in turn, can be assured of being cared for in my own old age. 'It is in giving that we receive.' Selfishness brings its own share of loneliness. Yes, indeed, the happiest people on earth are those who have time and space for others in their lives. In Christian terms, this is being a channel or an instrument, through whom the Lord continues his work on earth. Jesus said that he would not abandon us, he would not leave us orphan. We can, of course, end up that way, but that is our personal choice.

From the outset, I have to acknowledge this story as being one of my favourites from an O. Henry collection of short stories, even if I re-tell it from memory, and, therefore, take liberties with the original version. It is the story of a young couple, newly married, and deeply in love. They also happen to be unemployed, and very poor. It is right in the middle of the Great Depression in the US. They live in a one-room apartment in a big city. Although they are very poor, each has a personal possession that is very precious to each, and to both. The girl has the most beautiful long hair, that is the envy of all, and the pride of her husband. He has a beautiful gold pocket-watch that he inherited as a family heirloom, and his wife never stops admiring it.

It is Christmas eve. Both are deeply troubled, without telling the other. Each has a burning desire to buy the other a present for Christmas, but, of course, neither has the wherewithal to do anything about it. He has gone out, in the hope of getting some work, and, therefore some money, so that he can realise his dream. She is at home, and is experiencing a sense of hopelessness as the day goes on. Then, suddenly, a crazy thought strikes her. She grabs her coat, heads out the door, and heads for the nearest hair-dressing salon. She does a deal with the hairdresser, has all her hair cut off which could be used in natural-hair wigs, and, with the money, she heads down the street and buys a gold chain for her husband's gold watch. She knows that this is an act of craziness, but she loves him, and she just has to do something to express her love at such an important time of the year.

Back in the kitchen, she is preparing a few bits and pieces for the Christmas dinner. She is extremely nervous, as she convinced herself again and again that she did what she wanted to do, she did what she had to do. At the same time, of course, she was dreading her husband's reaction when he saw her without her flowing locks. She waited and waited, and it seemed forever. Finally, she heard footsteps on the stairs. Her husband had arrived home. Her heart was in her mouth, but she was determined to face the music. She kept speaking to herself, to reassure herself. And then the door opened, her husband entered, he looked at her, and his mouth fell open. 'Oh, honey, look ... look what I bought you', she said, as she opened the paper and showed him the chain for his gold watch. His mouth opened even wider, as he put his hand in his pocket, and handed her a small present. With shaking hands she opened it, to discover two beautiful ornamental gold 'slides' which he had bought for her to wear in her hair! He had sold his gold watch to buy them!

Giving till it hurts, or giving till it's gone? We all live in the world of reality, and yet, when we come across this kind of love, it stops us in our tracks! Despite the tendency to cynicism about such expressions of love, in a very materialistic world, I believe there is still a part of us that warms to such generosity. It is often said that we're not sure what to do with saints: Do we admire them, or imitate them? If nothing else, this story tells of two people who were very rich indeed, even if they had little or nothing of this world's goods.

'Where there's a will, there's a way' is more than just a cliché. Christianity lays great stress on the importance of good-will. Right from that first Christmas night it was proclaimed that there was peace available on earth to those of good-will. The very idea of will is worth looking at. It is more than just impulse or drive. It has to do with choices, decisions, and preferences. It often means choosing something over and above something else. A person of good-will is someone with a good heart, and a generous disposition. We are all familiar with the ideas of strong-willed, stubborn, iron-willed, and self-will run riot. The latter is most evidenced in addictive behaviour, where the addiction is calling the shots, and the individual is no longer in control.

To throw in the sponge, and give up, is the last resort, because it means walking away from the extraordinary resilience that is inherent in the human spirit. For the Christian, the only real sin is to lose hope. Victory over adversity is at the heart of the Christian message. By coming to join us on the journey, Jesus makes everything possible. 'Nothing is impossible to God', Mary was told, right at the beginning of the story. What is a problem for one person, can be seen by the Christian as an opportunity. Just as the incoming tide raises all the boats, so the generous love of these two young people might well lift the ideals of all of us.

Spirit and Breath of God, I ask you, please, to create a generous spirit within me. Please give me a giving heart, and an openness to others. By myself, Lord, I can so easily slip into my old narrow selfish ways. Please prevent that happening, Lord. I really do want to be a wholesome channel of love, hope, and life to those around me. Amen.

30. Jesus welcomes sinners

Jesus was condemned and killed because 'this man welcomes sinners, and even eats with them'. Whatever other pretences were made by way of accusation, that was the one that decided his fate. Especially, when he claimed he was God, and, therefore, that this is what God would do! That was a real shocker for the religious people of Jesus' day! God was all-holy, and how could anyone suggest that he would have anything to do with sinners, with those who were unclean, with those who didn't belong? The word 'welcome' means that your arrival gives me pleasure, makes me happy. We all have entered situations where we knew we were welcome, or we knew we weren't. Unfortunately, many of us, through bad, unloving experiences of the Sacrament of Reconciliation ('Confession') may not have been given this idea of a God who welcomes, a God who is pleased when I turn, or return, to him. It can be difficult, if not impossible, to undo the wrong impressions of those early experiences.

My earlier experiences of the Church was that it was a disaster when it came to sin, and to sinners! I could list over a dozen 'sins' we had back then, that are not sins at all now! The Church was big into excommunication, and into condemnation of individuals from the pulpit. Even some poor soul, in a dark moment of despair and hopelessness, who committed suicide, could not receive a church funeral, but, like some animal, was buried in an unmarked grave, in unconsecrated ground. I don't like going on about this, but, like the Holocaust, if we deny it, and pretend it never happened, then it is capable of happening all over again. Human nature can show up some tendencies that are frightening, at times, and when something that is evil is disguised as a good (religion) then it becomes even more frightening. Jesus' message is absolutely clear, and, even as he was dying on the cross, he was reaching out a hand of love, acceptance, and friendship to a sinner on one of the other crosses. Yes, indeed, he really does welcome sinners.

The *New York Post* carried the story of a group of young people travelling by bus to Fort Lauderdale in Florida. They were going on a vacation. Not long after leaving, they noticed the dark-skinned, middle-aged man, poorly dressed, and looking quite worried, as he sat slouched in his seat, with his head bowed. When the bus pulled in at a road-side cafe, everyone got out, except Vingo, as the young people had named him. The young people were curious about him. Where had he come from? Where was he going? Finally, one of them sat next to him, and said 'We're going to Florida. Would you like some of my coke?' He took a swig, and said 'Thank you.' After a while, he told his story.

He'd been in a New York prison for five years. 'While I was away I wrote to my wife, and told her I would be away for a long time, and if she couldn't take it, she should just forget about me, and get herself a life. I told her not to write or nothing, and she didn't. Not for four and a half years.' Then he said 'She's a wonderful woman, really good, really something.' 'And now you're going home, not sure what to expect?' the girl asked. 'Yes', he replied. 'You see, last week when my parole came through, I wrote to her again. I told her I would be coming by on the bus. As you come into Jacksonville, where we live, there's a big oak tree. I told her that if she'd take me back again, she could tie a yellow ribbon on the tree, and I'd get off the bus, and come home. If she didn't want me, forget it. No yellow ribbon, and I'd just keep going.'

The girl told the others, and soon they were all involved, looking at pictures of Vingo's wife, and children, and all getting more and more anxious, as they approached Jacksonville. There was a hushed mood on the bus. Vingo's face tightened. Then, suddenly, all the young people were out of their seats, screaming and shouting, crying and dancing. All except Vingo. He just sat there stunned, looking at the oak tree. It was covered with yellow ribbons, forty or fifty of them. The whole oak tree had been turned into one big welcome banner. As the young people shouted, and cried, Vingo rose from his seat, made his way to the front of the bus, smiled back at his young friends through a flood of tears, and got off.

We're all probably familiar with the song that was written about that incident. It is a song that can just as easily be seen as a hymn. Jesus was on this earth for thirty-three years. If, however, he had been on this earth for just three minutes, I believe he could have told us the core of his message with one of his most touching stories, the story of the Prodigal Son. Remember the following words of Jesus: 'I never say anything unless the Father tells me.' In other words, the Father told him to tell us that story; and the story of the Pharisee and the publican, as well as the parable of the hundred sheep, and his willingness to leave the ninety-nine, and search for the one that was lost. How clearer could I expect the message to be? If the Church misses out on this one, it misses the very purpose of its existence. The church has no other reason for its being than to represent Jesus Christ on this earth. The role of the Church is that of John the Baptist, to point to Jesus, to encourage people to follow him, and to get out of the way! The church has never been too good at keeping out of the way! Like John, the church must decrease, if Jesus is to increase.

Jesus tells the story of different debtors who owed differing sums of money. All were forgiven, freed of the debt, had the slate wiped clean. The question Jesus then asked was: 'Which of them would be most grateful, which of them would hold the lender in highest esteem?' In other words, the greatest sinners have the potential to become the most convicted followers of Jesus. The church tended to treat the sinner according to the gravity of the sin. Some sins were even outside the pale of forgiveness, and the person was excommunicated, and put beyond the boundaries of belonging. Once again, I have to say that this frightens me. It represents all that is worst about what we can presume to do with the message of Jesus. I just have to say it: How dare we! This, of course, is what happens when we take over, and try to run the show ourselves. Unless there is direct guidance from God's Spirit, human nature cannot be trusted. There is some sort of 'cussedness' in our nature, and obviously Jesus saw that we could never make it on our own. We certainly have within us the seeds of our own destruction. This same inclination also prompts us to attempt to destroy what the Lord wants to do for us. The church, after all, is made up of people, and that can be a dangerous ingredient, if left unguarded!

Yes, indeed, Jesus welcomes sinners, and he even eats with them. 'Happy are we who are called to his supper.' Everybody is called, but not everybody chooses to answer the call. Jesus told several stories about people being invited to a meal, and how, one after another, each found some excuse for not showing up. It must surely be one of the greatest sufferings for someone who ends up in hell, to see then just how available everything was, and how, for some perverse and insane reason, some other road had been chosen.

> *Heavenly Father, thank you for sending Jesus to tell us that there are yellow ribbons all over heaven whenever any of us turns back to you. You are the Prodigal Father, with your arms opened wide to welcome home the child who has strayed. Father, I ask for an outpouring of your Spirit, so that my heart may be touched, my hope may be strengthened, and my openness to reconciliation and wholeness might be increased. Amen.*

31. To do what Jesus did

Scripture tells us that Jesus 'came to do and to teach'. He did something, like washing the apostles' feet, and then he told them to do the same for each other. His was a hands-on approach right from the beginning, and his instructions were totally and plainly practical. He spoke to the prostitute, he touched the leper, he ran around with sinners. His purpose was not to deliberately upset anyone, but to act and behave as he honestly believed he should. Up to that time every single dimension of life for the Jewish people was bound up in rule and ritual. This even covered the number of steps one was allowed take on a Sabbath. The rule was uppermost, was in control, and it got to the stage where people's very reason for being was to keep those rules. And then Jesus comes along saying 'The Sabbath was made for people, not people for the Sabbath'. Such phrases from Jesus must really have ruffled a few feathers. The Scribes were a group whose full-time task was to interpret the law, and the full-time task of the Pharisees was to apply the law. Their religion was nothing more than a collection of laws, and, by having laws decide whether a person was good or evil, it meant that God wasn't too directly involved in any role, except that of spectator. Without ever sitting down and planning an over-all strategy, it was just another very clear example of human nature taking over and running the show. Original sin in yet another form. The more I go on in life, the more convinced I am that, left to itself, human nature drifts towards becoming God! This is strange, in a way; strange, as in 'funny'. You see, the plan of salvation is about rescuing us from ourselves, and enabling us come and share in the life of the Trinity. In other words, it's God's idea that we should be raised to such heights. What is funny, while being both stupid and sad, is that we are more than willing to assume this elevated state all on our own, and by our own efforts!

In the western world, we often joke about the Japanese being able to produce a cheaper and smaller version of any product the West can produce! Probably made of plastic, and cast in a mould, but a very good imitation. That's what I have in mind when I see humans trying to do what only God can do. Creating and re-creating is God's work, and only God can do God's work. Jesus followed this line with total commitment. He never said anything unless the Father told him to tell us. 'I never do anything of myself ... My very life is to do the will of him who sent me.' Right here is a veritable treasure of spirituality, if one dare use such material terms to describe such sublime riches. What I mean here is this: With all the tip-toeing we do around this God of infinite mystery, we can actually listen to what Jesus says and does, and come to know quite a great deal about this God! Jesus was told to tell us the stories about the Prodigal Son, the Pharisee and the Publican, the lost sheep, the weeds among the wheat, etc. I contend that these stories reveal the heart of God, and, in its sheer simplicity, that is awesome. There is something in us that insists on making God out to be very complicated, and beyond comprehension! However, when God decided to come on earth, he came in the weakest possible human form. By making that starting-point our starting-point, we have endless treasures of revelation of sheer simplicity in every page of the gospels that follow. What extraordinary graces await those who listen again, with open and unprejudiced hearts, to exactly what Jesus said, and who watch yet again exactly what Jesus did.

It was a parish in Ireland. The parish priest was going off for the day, and the curate was going to attend to a funeral later that day. The parish priest returned that night, and dropped by to say hello to the curate, and to enquire how the day, and, particularly, the funeral had gone. He was quite laid back about the whole thing, not expecting any great problem to arise. He was told that Mrs Robinson was there, who was a Protestant, but, of course, he had expected that, because she had been a good friend of the deceased. He was on his feet, however, when the curate said that she had come up for Communion. 'What did you do? What did you do?' he kept repeating, with his blood pressure rising by the second. 'I didn't know what to do', replied the curate. 'She was about three away from me before I noticed her.' 'What did you do?' shrieked the parish priest, as the veins began to stand out on his forehead. 'Well,' said the curate, 'I was faced with a dilemma, and I had to make a quick decision.' 'What decision? What decision did you make?' asked the parish priest, now on the point of having a stroke. 'I felt that I was caught off guard, I had to make a quick decision, and so I made the decision to do what I believe Jesus would do in the circumstances.' The parish priest emitted a roar of anguish, as he gasped 'Oh, no! Oh, my God, you didn't!'

To do what Jesus would do in the circumstances was probably totally contrary to 'what we do around here.' How often have I heard that phrase! 'We don't preach at funerals here.' 'We don't go in for girl Mass servers here.' 'We don't have any of that hurdy-gurdy guitar-stuff in this church.' I remember hearing of an Afro-American man standing outside a church for whites in the one of the southern states of the US. He would not, of course, be allowed enter, but he loved the singing, and he was happy enough to stand outside and listen. Who came along but Jesus, who asked him why he hadn't gone into the church. The man explained that he would not be allowed, and there was nothing he could do about it. Jesus replied 'I know how you feel. I myself have been trying to get into that church for years.' Jesus was asked what the law said, and he replied that we should love the Lord with all our hearts, and love our neighbour as ourselves. Later on he went one step further when he told them that they were to love one another as he loved them. In other words, to do what Jesus would do.

Jesus was quite predictable in what he did. When there was a choice between a person and a rule, the person always took precedence. 'The law says to you ..., but I say to you...' He was so much more into the law of love than the love of law. This put him on a sure and certain crash course with the religious leaders of his day. Enforcing rules gives people control over others, just as slavish adherence to rules provides a sense of security and stability to others. 'The Lord alone you should obey, and him only shall you serve'. I'm always in trouble whenever I allow others have control over me. My own Church has used laws quite effectively for centuries to control the lives of others. This seems strange, when we speak of Jesus coming to set us free! Rules and laws are for protecting people, not for controlling them. We need laws, because who wants to live in a lawless society? During my years of teaching, I always found that pupils actually liked a school in which there was discipline, and, if the application of rules lapsed in their school, they would soon move elsewhere. Jesus was not at all against rules. However, he certainly was against making the law an end in itself, where people were there just to uphold the law. He was a people-first person all the way.

Lord Jesus, save us from ourselves! If there is any particular grace I would ask for here, it is: Lord, please help me, through the work of your Spirit in my heart, to put you above all beliefs, all religions, all churches. Please Lord, don't ever allow me get lost in law, and lose sight of love. All I ask, Lord, is that I might always be open, ready, and available to do things your way, as you would wish. Thank you, Lord. Amen.

32. Praying from the heart

Over the main altar of the basilica in Assisi are the words *'Si cor non orat, in vanum lingua laborat'* (If the heart is not praying, the tongue labours in vain). The organ God gave me to pray with is the heart, not the tongue. 'These people honour me with their lips, but their hearts are far from me.' When I come before God, I can always be sure that he looks at the heart, and he listens to the heart. If I speak from the heart, I speak to the heart, and that is true of all conversations, including prayer. Prayer actually becomes much easier when it comes from the heart. Imagine a huge beach, with the tide coming in. I am the beach, and the Lord is the tide. Prayer is what happens to me, when I put myself in the way of it, as it were.

When I speak of the heart, I speak of that part of me where I am my most authentic; that inner Child me, that part of me that is behind the masks, the barriers, the barricades, and the games I play. It is said that when I go to sleep, the ego is off guard, and that Inner Child comes out to play, and we call that dreams. There is a freedom about dreams, where anything is liable to happen, and where I am not in control. It's interesting to note that when dreams bring us into situations where we have lost control, they usually become nightmares! People have been called 'dreamers' because they dared to be different, to try something new, to go down the road less travelled. They are people who do not live in their heads, and, therefore, are not able to stand back with cool detachment, and be seen to have everything under control. They are not calculating, they give without counting the cost, and they generally invest themselves totally in the now. Because of the centrality of the heart, they are said to be warm people, to be genuine, to be authentic. Prayer becomes so much easier when I'm honest. No need to impress God with long conversations, or to act as some sort of Reuters correspondent, keeping God informed of everything that's going on down here on earth! It is not enjoyable to be in the company of such people, and it is not totally unreal to suggest that God might also find that to be so! There is a certain 'free-fall' about prayer, and this happens when it is accepted that prayer is actually what God does, rather than anything I do. If it is something that I do, then it can become very predictable, and, of course, often boring. When I was a child I learned that 'Prayer is a raising of the mind and heart to God ...' I like that now, even if I failed to understand it at the time. Prayer is a gesture, a statement of attitude, rather than a multiplicity of words. There is, of course, a vast difference between praying, and saying prayers.

There are many simple and practical examples of prayer in the gospels. The cry came from the heart, and Jesus was 'rooted' to the spot, as it were. Such cries always reach the heart of God, who is full of compassion and love. If they had anything in common it is that they were directed towards the one person who was capable of answering them. When I'm on the broad of my back, there's only one way to look, and that's up!

> Three priests were having a very intellectual debate on prayer. They discussed the merits of different stances, or bodily postures during prayer. One spoke strongly about being on one's knees, because that signified humility, reverence, and the proper attitude of the creature before the creator. A second argued strongly for the lotus position, legs crossed, back upright, hands opened out on lap. This suggested a sign of availability, of 'Speak, Lord, your servant is listening.' The third was very definite that the correct posture at prayer was that adopted by Jesus himself, who 'cast his eyes up to heaven.' Surely no one could improve on the very method Jesus himself used.

> There was an electrician working nearby, and he could not help hearing this profound debate. He was hesitant, but he chose to speak up, and contribute his little bit. 'Far be it from me to enter into a debate on prayer with 'men of the cloth'! However, I just want to tell you what my own experience has been. I never thought much about right or wrong postures at prayer. Then, one day, I found myself hanging by one leg from an electric pole,

in the middle of a thunderstorm, after the ladder had slipped. I
cried out to God, in that position, and, do you know something,
he heard me!'

To involve the body in prayer, of course, is a good thing, but only
when it helps the inner me to be more present, and more open.
Comfortable, relaxed positions help to move the focus away from
the body, and there is a much better chance of inner availability. An
uncomfortable physical position can serve as a distraction. The
amount of words used is not at all an issue, as I'm sure the man sus-
pended from the electric pole wasn't into delivering any lengthy
speeches! There can be as many physical postures as there are people, but there is only one correct inner disposition This is a sense of
good-will and of availability, and whatever happens then is totally
up to God. I give God the time and the space, and I leave the rest to
him. Again and again, in these reflections, I find myself returning to
the central theme of disposition and attitude. Right from the very
outset of the Messianic mission, it was stated clearly: Peace on earth
to those of good-will. It is not about holiness, perfection, rules,
virtue, or performance. It is about an inner disposition. How often
we find ourselves going through the motions, as it were, as we
speak or relate to others. At a funeral I could wear my 'mourning
face', and say all the words of comfort, and not really have any
great feeling one way or another. Generally speaking, it's easy
enough to know who is sincere, and who is just going through the
motions. Insincerity on any level is disquieting, but it surely
becomes anathema when it enters into prayer. As if God cannot see
what's in the heart, or what is lacking there! The more I reflect on
prayer, the more convinced I am that there is very little one can really
say about it. (Says I, while writing more pages!) What I mean,
though, it that I can expound on all the theories, but the necessary
disposition has to come from within the person. No other person
can give that, or ensure that it's there. When I was a child, I was
taught many many prayers, but I don't remember ever being taught
how to pray. I even believe now that it's probably impossible to
teach someone to pray. I can explain, illustrate, or demonstrate, but
the door of the human heart has only one handle, and that is on the
inside.

It is more than a mistake, because it is intrinsically wrong, to speak of prayer without reference to the Holy Spirit. All that I have tried in share in this reflection is directly the work of the Spirit. It is the Spirit who changes our words and thoughts into prayer, and, if the Spirit is not in our words, then we're only talking to ourselves. Peter O'Toole, in a movie called The Working Class, is in a psychiatric hospital, and his problem is that he thinks he's God. To humour him, the psychiatrist asks him when he first discovered he was God. He replied 'I was praying and praying for years and years, and then, one day, I woke up and discovered that I was only talking to myself'! There are alot of people who spend alot of time talking to themselves, and they call it prayer. Like any other dimension of my relationship with God, it is very important that I give first place at all times to the divine initiative, and never allow myself turn that into human endeavour.

Spirit and Breath of God, I think of you as my Spiritual Director when it comes to prayer. I look to you to turn my thoughts, words, and deeds into prayer. I ask you, please, to inspire me, to anoint me, to empower me, so that I can grow in my openness to the every-minute possibility of prayer. Please give me a praying heart. Amen.

33. The presence of the Lord

The Jesus of history and the Christ of faith is the same person. Jesus was God among his people, and he continues to live among us. The person is the same, even if the name may vary. His name is Jesus, which means Saviour, because that was, and is, his primary function. Because he is the Messiah and the Anointed of God, he is entitled to be called Christ, which means The Holy One, The Anointed One. The full name of Jesus Christ gives a more complete picture in a tradition where the name given tells much of the person bearing that name. Scripture attaches great importance to the idea of a person's name. The early believers were even referred to as believers in The Name. St Paul tells us that there is no other name given to us, under heaven, whereby we can be saved, and at the name of Jesus, every knee should bend. At various times, and in divers ways God revealed himself as being present to his people. He was in the burning bush, the cooling cloud, the whispering breeze. The people were in such awe of God that they would never say his name. They built tabernacles, and Holy of Holies in the temple, and they believed that God made his home there. Such places were unapproachable and untouchable to the ordinary mortal. To touch the tabernacle would result in the person being struck dead, and the High Priest, and he alone, could enter the Holy of Holies on one occasion each year.

The coming of Jesus, then, was something extraordinary in every way. There is no way the religious leaders of those times could accept this truth. This was preposterous, and a blasphemy. It seems strange that a God who was considered to be infinite, was deemed incapable of coming down to the level of human nature, something which he himself had created in the first place. Even today, one can hear references which give a hint that, somehow, Jesus was not really a down-to-earth God. We may read Paul's words about Jesus being like us in all things, and having being tempted exactly as we are, even if he did not sin. I take that to mean that there is not one human struggle I myself have experienced that Jesus himself did not also encounter during his life. I even believe that if I have a weakness that he did not personally struggle with, and overcome, then I just cannot be saved.

The more I come to understand and appreciate the reality of the Jesus of history, the more I come to relate in a more realistic way with the Christ of faith. We speak of the same Jesus. He is just as down-to-earth now as he ever was. The gospels certainly reveal his thinking, his teaching, and his attitudes. No other person in history has had so much written about him, has had his every word and act analysed in fine detail, and is still being looked at from all possible angles. All of this, of course, could be nothing more than history, if we do not cross the bridge from our knowledge of Jesus, to our faith in him.

> It was a local wedding. The girl in particular was entering into the preparations with total commitment. It was not going to be just a carbon copy of any other wedding she herself had attended. It was her wedding, and it would have her own special stamp on it. One of the things that bothered her was how best to link up the church part of the wedding with the celebrations in the hotel. There were occasions in the past when she had felt she was at two different weddings. She approached the priest doing the wedding with a suggestion. Was there any possibility that they could drink a toast around the altar after the Mass, and this would serve as a bridge to the celebrations in the hotel? The priest was fairly laid-back, and accommodating, and, because the wedding was going to take place on the parish priest's weekly day off, he saw no problem with that.
>
> It was the day of the wedding. Everything was going well. The Mass ended, the forms were signed, the unending photo session was under way. Then the glasses were produced, the wine was poured, and a genuine and lively sense of celebration was in the air. And then, lo and behold, the parish priest walked in! He had returned unexpectedly to collect something he had forgotten. To

say he was shocked is putting it mildly! He demanded to know what was going on. The family were quick in passing responsibility to the priest, so the parish priest went gunning for him. He knew he was caught. He had no way out, so he decided to be as matter-of-fact as possible. He just couldn't see what the problem was. 'What about Cana of Galilee?' he ventured, in desperation. 'Look at all the wine they had at that wedding' 'This is a totally different situation', fumed the parish priest. 'How can you possibly make such a comparison? Cana of Galilee was an entirely different situation. The Blessed Sacrament wasn't there'!

I am being totally honest when I say that I'm really enjoying writing these reflections, even when some of them are written with tongue in cheek! There's many a truth spoken in jest! Even if we can laugh at some of the things we do, it is hoped that we may see just how ridiculous it is to continue doing those things. The very aura that has come to surround what we call The Blessed Sacrament may well have stripped Jesus of a great deal of what he brought into our human situation. Surely there's no more suitable place for a real celebration than in the presence of the Lord. After all, don't God's people gather there to celebrate every day, and, incidentally, there's wine involved. I sometimes refer to what I call 'the transforming power of holy water'. People come across from the parking lot towards the church. They are chatting, smiling, waving at each other. It can be a wonderful aspect of the Sunday morning. There are enquiries about a sick member of the family, or whether the other is going to the game today. Then, suddenly, once the finger touches the holy water, something happens! All life seems to drain away, the face becomes firm and fixed, and the people on either side cease to exist. At the sign of peace you find yourself holding what feels like the tail of a fish, some lifeless thing. This state continues until the finger goes back into the holy water on the way out. And then, hurrah, we're all human beings again! I know that is exaggerated, but there sure is alot of truth in it. If Jesus took on our humanity, then the more human I can become, the more open to him I will be.

There is a place, obviously, for candles, flowers, incense, and lights. This can be a form of prayer, an expression of worship. Many a time in the gospel, someone came along, saw Jesus as an everyday ordinary human being, and yet that person saw beneath all that, and fell prostrate before him. All of that is very good, and it is part of the relationship between creator and creature. Referring back to the holy water effect, the only ones not effected are the children. I am not at all advocating that children should be allowed run riot in church! What I am saying, however, is that theirs is the nearest thing to natural behaviour that might be seen in church. The priest who tells the mother to remove the disruptive kid is nothing short of an abomination, and it is he who should be removed! Jesus dealt very firmly with that in the gospel when the apostles tried to get the mothers to take their kids elsewhere.

> *Spirit and Breath of God, I know only too well that I am capable of being as narrow as the next, in some area of life. Please help me. Through your work in me, please open my heart to everything and anything that is of God, and free me from the deceptions that set limits to all that. Amen.*

34. Each has a part to play

Life is, indeed, a mystery to be lived. I offer some of the following images for your consideration. I am standing up in a very tall box, whose sides prevent me seeing anything in the distance. My world is very limited, and I experience a sense of being, literally, 'boxed in'. At the moment of death, the sides of the box fall away, I look around, and I gasp with wonder. Another image is a beautiful oil painting of a magnificent country scene, extending from one end of a wall to the other. The problem is that the painting is covered with sacking, with a tiny opening, about one inch square. Through that opening I can see some grass, and part of some trees. At the moment of death, the sacking is whipped away, and, once again, I am left gasping in wonder at the beauty. What is also evident is that my little one inch square is part of this total picture. If it were missing, the picture would be the poorer. I cannot pretend to understand life, but I can draw certain conclusions. God is a God of love, and his actions are never purposeless, capricious, or at the whim of the moment. I like to think that his plan is magnificent, all-embracing, all-inclusive. If I ever begin believing in coincidences or accidents, then I'll have to stop believing in God. I believe that coincidences are God's way of preserving his anonymity.

While being totally incapable of having a bird's-eye view of life, I must say I find great consolation in the thought that such a view is available, even to God. Not only that, but when, like an ordinance survey map, I look at a particular detail, I see myself very definitely programmed into the over-all scenario. There is a vast difference between faith and hindsight! I know, that, when I die, I'll be able to look back and see that everything God allowed happen to me in life was seen by him as having a potential for good, whether I availed of that or not. Even my sins, brokenness, and failures are the source of any compassion I may have. As I said I will see this with hindsight, after I die. The person of faith, however, accepts that fact now, and so, there is a constant awareness of God's plan and purpose for me, even when things are not going the way I think they should. 'All things work for good for those who love God', says Paul. It is this kind of faith that enabled someone like Francis of Assisi to praise and thank God when things went well, and when things went against him. I often think that there's an atheist hidden within all of us. If I could only get the proof first, then, of course, I would believe! I am asked, however, to do the living, the trusting, and the walking now, and get the proof later on. Such trust in God is a direct response to love, and it is reasonable to accept that this is impossible for someone who is still not convinced of God's love and purpose for us.

Each of us has a song to sing, a task to perform, a role to play, and I am the only person who can fulfil my calling. My life is unique, my purpose is personal, within the larger community of the Body of Christ. St Paul tells us that some are called to be teachers, some preachers, some prophets. We are different members of the same body, and when one member functions with health, the whole body benefits. For a body to function, it is necessary that each member be different, that each performs some particular task. If the eyes do not function, then the hands and the ears have to take over, and make up the difference. Only when the members function as they ought is the body complete. Within the over-all plan of God, none of us is here without a purpose, and a pre-ordained part in the divine economy of life.

> There were three young trees growing together in a forest. They were young, healthy, and ambitious. They compared their dreams. One wanted to be part of the structure of a castle or palace, so would be a spectator in the lives of the high and mighty of society. The second wanted to end up as the mast in one of the tall ships, sailing around the world with a great sense of adventure. The third hoped to end up as part of some public monument, where the public would stop, admire, and photograph.

> Years passed by, and all three were cut down. The first was chopped up, and parts of it were put together to form a manger for a stable in Bethlehem. The second was cut down, and the

trunk was scooped out, and formed into a boat, which was launched on the sea of Galilee. The third was cut into sections, two of which were put together, to form a cross on Calvary. Each had a unique and special part to play in the one great story of redemption.

There is nothing wrong with ambition, there is nothing wrong with having a dream. As we listen to Jesus praying in the garden, he asks for something, but concludes with the words 'Nevertheless, not my will, but yours be done.' To pray like this is to pray with the heart and the mind of Christ. It is not fatalism, stoicism, pre-determinism. The simple truth is that only God knows what is best for us, and, so, it makes sense to leave the final word with him. If God were sadistic and cruel, he would answer every prayer we utter, and then have a good laugh! We must surely ask for many things that are not for our good, but, thanks to God's great love, we do not receive what is not for our benefit.

When it comes to God there is an over-all sense of good. Like the bricks in a house, they all form part of the structure, whether one in down near the ground, and the other is up near the roof. Each of the trees in our story played a separate and important part in the unfolding of the same drama. Each part was separate, just as each call is unique. It is very interesting to see just how Jesus called people in the gospel. He called them one by one. He didn't ask the thousands who received the loaves and fishes to follow him. It is also interesting, by the way, to note that he never sent them out in ones. On the only two occasions when someone ventured out on his own, one denied him, and the other betrayed him. Each individual is a very unique reflection of some dimension of God. No one person (or Church, for that matter) can claim to have a monopoly on God. God is even bigger than the sum of the parts.

There is a sort of X-factor in our lives. By that I mean that, despite all God's plans and purposes, not much can happen without my co-operation. I know it sounds crazy that I can end up frustrating God's eternal plans for me, but I believe that to be the case. Another word for that X-factor is 'Yes', and it is only when that is forthcoming from me that God's Spirit can move in, as it were, and Incarnation begin. Without that 'Yes', God's plan for me is still-born. Life is a gift, given for the service of others. Each of the trees thought of life as something from which each could earn a position of importance. That is not necessarily bad, because life can be very rewarding. However, as in the story, what they are remembered for is what each was able to give to the unfolding of God's plan of salvation and redemption. The extraordinary thing about this, as with each and every life, is that life gave a return away beyond the wildest dream, and that came directly from the role of service.

Lord Jesus, I offer myself to you for whatever task you have for me in the building of your kingdom. Please keep me firm in my belief and trust, even when I fail to see where I fit in, or what purpose I serve. This is your idea, Lord, it is your work, it is your plan and purpose. Thanks, Lord, for deciding to involve and include me. Amen.

35. Being touched by God

'Touch' is a word that has many meanings and connotations. There is the physical touch of reaching out with a finger, and making contact with something or someone. There is the 'nice touch', where the contact is not physical, but the effect of an action makes contact with the other, emotionally or psychologically. We speak of a 'touch' of something, from nerves, regret, guilt, or the common cold, all meaning some small degree. The word 'touch', as I use it in this reflection, is to look at how God touches us, and how we are touched by God. To speak of something as being very 'touching', is to imply that it went beneath the exterior surface of the physical, and made contact with us on a deeper personal level. I think of Jesus as the Father reaching out to touch and embrace us. Jesus assures us that when we return to the Father, there is a big hug waiting for us.

For very religious people, there are always people and things that are untouchable. They are deemed not to be good, and, therefore, capable of contamination. Among the religious leaders of Jesus' day there were many such untouchables. Lepers figured at the top of that list. Outcasts, sinners, prostitutes, possessed, and the dead, all belonged to that long list. Jesus touched each and every one of these. It is not possible for us today to fully understand the extent of the shock and scandal this would have caused among the religious leaders. The only explanation they could come up with was that he was possessed, because only someone with an evil spirit could so deliberately flout the law in so many different ways. While not accepting it as true, it almost looked as if Jesus flaunted a disrespect for the very basics of the law. It is not possible to understand this properly without special reference to Incarnation. Jesus actually took on a body, with hands, feet, and voice, so that he could physically make contact with us in every way, and not in some abstract esoteric manner. He hugged the little children, he took hold of the hand of the dead daughter of Jairus, or the son of the widow of Naim, and he reached out and touched the leper. It is not possible to exaggerate how extraordinary and different these actions were. Today, we speak of a hands-on policy, where someone is described as being in everyday contact with the details of a situation. Jesus certainly had a hands-on approach, and he introduced a whole new ministry of touch.

This ministry is a very important one. We see it in action during prayers for healing, or while accompanying the dying. It is powerful during times of bereavement, or great stress, when words fail hopelessly to convey what cannot be put into words. It is at the core of nurturing for babies and young children, who, even when asleep, are gaining from the personal touch of being held in the mother's arms. How often I have encouraged mothers to place a hand of blessing on the fevered brow of a sick child, allowing the love in the heart flow through the arm to the body of the sick one. This form of healing is very real, practical, simple, and available to all who are capable of love. The feelings of the heart are transmitted through the touch. The love, the longings, the prayers within the heart are transferred over to the other. When I pray with someone who is sick, I love to have someone present who, through family or other relationship, can claim to really love the sick person. The touch of such a person is powerfully healing. The power is not ours. We are just channels or instruments of that power. We are transformers, not generators. God is the source of all love, healing, and power. When we put ourselves in contact with God, all that he is can then flow through us. The ministry of touch has special meaning at such times, when we actually become touch-persons for God, who has no other hands, feet, or voice but ours.

I remember being profoundly moved by the unfolding of events in Romania, at the fall of the dictatorship there some years ago. It was at the beginning of the availability of the satellite news channels in these parts, and I sat up all night, catching the news every hour, on the hour. That, for me, was a night to remember.

This caused me to have a particular interest in events in that

country since then. My interest was heightened enormously a
year later, when I knew a young girl who went out there, as one
of a group, to work in the many orphanages that were discovered or uncovered, after the horrible evil clouds had been dis-
pelled. She has a heart as big as her body, and her first weeks
there was one continuous nightmare. The first two things that
struck her as she entered an orphanage was the stench, and the
silence. The babies were living at a level unacceptable in the animal kingdom. Matters of toilet were totally neglected, and when
babies cry, and no one comes to comfort, they eventually stop
crying. At the approach of an adult the babies were seen to shiver
with terror, because they had no experience whatever of being
touched, let alone nursed. They resembled frightened young
wild rabbits. It took hours and hours of painful patient sensitivity
to allay those fears, and to permit a human touch, without trau-
ma. It was a very long process to gain their confidence, and to be
able to approach without generating terror. Day after day, the
work continued. It was weeks later before the babies began to
relax, and to yield to the sense of being touched, and being held.
Mary, that was her name, still speaks with tears in her eyes,
when she describes the sheer joy of getting a baby to the point of
lifting little arms, asking to be lifted, and held. Such moments
made it all worth while for the girls who had come to respond to
the plight of these little innocent ones.

No words of mine could ever do justice to the reality of such a
hell-hole, or to the sheer joy of making the eventual break-
through. If these girls did nothing else in their lives, they had
experienced something that few others could ever imagine.

I often think of Mary and those other girls, when I think of how God
wants to draw close to us, to hold us, to love us. Unfortunately,
even a God of love must experience a tremor of fear when he tries to
make such personal contact with us. He reaches out both hands, in
Jesus, and he genuinely wants us to experience his hug. The saint is
not the person who loves God. Rather is she the person who is totally
convinced that God loves her. When I listened to Mary's description of how she longed to lift those babies straightaway, nurse
them, and love them, and the painful frustration of the gradual
induction that had to precede such an achievement, I thought of

how God must feel when he tries to reach out to us. Scripture speaks of God wanting to take us in his arms, as a mother would a child, to hold us close to him, to press his cheek against ours. I can never fully understand the origin of our fears, but it surely must have something to do with alienation, resulting from original sin. 'Greater love than this no one can have ...' God has done all he can to bridge the gap, and he awaits our response to his invitation to return to him with all our hearts. 'If your sins were as scarlet, I will make them white as snow.' 'I will never forget you my people. I have carved you on the palms of my hands.'

Heavenly Father, I thank you that you have done everything possible to convince me of your love, and of how close you want to come to us. Please, Father, remove anything from within me that would limit that closeness, that would hold you at bay, or that would prevent my openness to your hug. Thank you, Father. Amen.

36. The enemy within

I don't think it's fair to blame the devil for all the evil in the world! A temptation is not a temptation if it doesn't appeal to some inner appetite. It must strike a chord within my spirit, or like a fish looking at an uninteresting bait, I'll just pass it by. For example, a temptation for one person would not be a temptation for another. From earliest childhood this is evident. There are children, and money could be left lying around the place, and it would never be touched. Then there are others and it is not safe to leave anything like money unguarded. I know this has alot to do with very early training and formation. I do, however, believe that there is some element of nature as well as nurture in the two different reactions. A temptation is like dangling some precious ornament outside the window of my mind, to provoke some reaction within. Again, using the image of the fish, I could rise to the bait instinctively, or I could be totally indifferent. I'm sure we all have known families where a teetotaller and an alcoholic came from the same nesting place.

There is an exact parallel between our weaknesses, our temptations, and our witness. The temptation is always tailored to the weakness. No point in trying to tempt a strict teetotaller by putting a glass of whiskey in front of him! He's just not interested. On the other hand, our greatest witness comes from our weakness. In other words, the greatest witness an alcoholic can give is to walk sober down the main street of his own town. For his brother to do that would not be much of a witness, because he is expected to do that, anyhow! The witness value comes from a weakness that is seen to be superseded by God's grace. 'See what marvellous things the Lord has done for me' is the message of my witness.

Our basic problem is that we all have an enemy within. As a direct result of original sin, there is some sort of basic rebelliousness within, that is always ready to sell out to the enemy. The temptation is always tempting to that part of us. It includes our drives, appetites, impulses, and compulsions. My body doesn't need the alcohol, the nicotine, the food, the thrill. A doctor who specialises in health through proper diet told me one time that it is the two-thirds extra we eat, which we don't need, that keeps other doctors in business! The 'hunger' we experience has more to do with what best can be described as a hole in the heart, an emptiness within. The problem here is that this can be filled and sated only by God. That is the way we are created, and nothing short of God can meet that need.

> The Great Wall of China is one of the wonders of the world. It is said to be the only human-made structure on earth that can be seen from the moon. The cost and the effort that went into building it just boggles the mind. When it was finished, the people relaxed. They knew they were safe. Nobody could possibly attack them now. It was impossible to either climb over, or penetrate their superb protecting wall, and behind it they were safe.

> But their enemies got through easily. How? They simply bribed one of the gate-keepers! He opened the gate, and they came through unhindered.

So much for human endeavour to protect itself, or to ensure its own safety! There is something deep within the human psyche that's capable of great good or of terrible evil. In these days we are used to international forces entering a country or region, and attempting to act as peace-keepers between two or more warring forces. There is something in us that makes it impossible for us to police our own welfare. Sometimes this is seen as self-will run riot, at other times it is simply insane behaviour. Alongside the extraordinary potential for magnificence, we also possess the seeds of our own destruction. The actual work of redemption, of reclaiming, takes place at our level, where we're at, but the power to do that must come from something above us. This is what is called The Higher Power. Only God can lift us out of the quicksand of our own selfishness. All human effort, and there has been mountains and mountains of such endeavours made over the years, all attempts on our part to change the human condition is doomed to fail, by its very nature. Human nature is mortal, therefore, every human effort is mortal, has but a limited life-span. By its very nature, it cannot last. The Great Wall of China would be capable of protecting the people only for a certain length of time. It may be around for a long time now, and it may still be around centuries from now, but it possesses nothing of infinity or of eternity. The very world, of which it is a part, will, itself, come to an end. 'Remember, man/woman, that thou art dust ...' 'Unless the Lord build the house (Wall?), in vain do the builders labour.'

I am not at all pessimistic about human nature! I just need to stress the simple truth, again and again, that human nature is hide-bound by its own limitations. It is unrealistic to expect a stone to burst into blossom, or an apple to start talking! There is nothing wrong with the stone, or the apple, as long as each remains exactly what it is. None of us expects these things to be anything other than what they are created to be. The same common sense should apply to our expectations of human nature. At this level of our consideration, however, something extraordinary can enter the formula. Call it pride, call it blindness, or call it simply original sin. God is used to usurpers of all sizes and descriptions, all eager to take over his position, and do his work for him! However, God will be still there, even when there's not the slightest remaining evidence of the Great Wall of China! The main problem we can experience here, of course, is that we are dealing with an eternal truth, and when it comes to something like this, only God can implant it in our minds, and imprint it on our spirit. We can read all the books in the world, and have the truths and theories coming out our ears, and then turn around, and act as if that is not so! No alcoholic ever stopped drinking, simply by reading a book about the evils of alcoholism! In fact, I have met a few bad alcoholics who are highly qualified to write such a book themselves, if they could only stay sober long enough to put pen to paper!

I said earlier that I am not at all pessimistic about humanity. I would argue a totally opposite line, in fact. I contend that, once I accept the realistic limits of my nature, I am then free and ready to enter into limitless life, a life beyond my wildest dreams. My own stupid stubbornness can imprison me in the solitary confinement of my own powerlessness. I don't know how to break out, but I am convinced that, some day, one day, today, I will succeed! I sometimes think that God smiles rather than cries when he watches us, because we must surely come across as being more stupid than evil!

Spirit and Breath of God, I look to you constantly to be reassured that I do not fall foul of the evil spirit, or of my own human spirit. I am very certain that I wouldn't survive long, if you were not there. I am only too conscious of the enemy within. That is why I call on you, please, to fill up every empty space within my whole being, so that all of that potential for evil is displaced. Thank you, Lord. Amen.

37. The Language of God

The word language can be misleading, because it comes from *lingua*, the Latin for tongue. Language, however, properly understood, is a method of expression. Now there are as many methods of expression as there are people. For example, we are all familiar with sign language, with the language of love that can be communicated through a look, and, indeed, the language of hatred, which can also be communicated through a look. In other words, if I think of language as something to do with the use of words, I am seriously limiting its usage and its implication. We all have come across people who could be described as being brilliant communicators. Some were teachers, some preachers, some writers, some artists, some musicians, some poets, etc., etc. The list goes on and on. Communication is a wonderful skill. It is multi-facial, many-sided, and, at its lowest, if it is not at least two-way, it is no-way! Whatever form my language takes, the secret is to ensure that it comes from the heart. The heart is my transmitter, and, when I communicate from the heart, I communicate to the heart. At this time in history, we are living in an age of communication. Every year sees some new development in the field of communications. This has its own in-built dangers, because we can come to rely on *something* to do the work of *someone*. I met a man recently who told me he had sent birthday greetings to his son, from his computer to his son's computer! I am not questioning the sincerity of the act, but, considering that both were just a few miles apart, I wondered were we on the way towards losing the personal contact.

The language of God is difficult to define in our dictionaries. It is impossible to encompass the full meaning of the word love in a dictionary. To quote a phrase I have used more than once in these reflections: For those who do not understand, no words are possi-

155

ble, and for those who do understand, no words are necessary. I speak of communication as some sort of chemistry, an electric current that crosses space, and makes contact. I'm sure there must be millions of books on prayer, scattered all over the globe. This is all very well, and it certainly serves a purpose. I would contend, however, that the person who makes the most meaningful contact with God, is the one who is most open to God communicating with her. There is an old Irish saying 'God spoke first', and there is great wisdom hidden within that. When I was a child, my father used endeavour to put me in my place (without much success!) by reminding me that he was on this earth before me!

> There is a legend about an African boy called Emmanuel, who was always asking questions. One day he asked the question 'What language does God speak?' No one could answer him. He travelled all over his own country with the same question, but still did not receive an answer. Eventually, he set off to other continents, in search of an answer to his question. For a long time he had no success. At last, one night, he came to a village called Bethlehem, and, as there was no room in the local inns, he went outside the village, in search of a shelter for the night. He came to a stable, and he saw that it was occupied by a couple, and their child. He was about to turn away when the young mother spoke. 'Welcome, Emmanuel. We've been expecting you.' The boy was amazed that the woman knew his name. He was even more amazed when she went on to say 'For a long time now, you have been searching the world to find out what language God speaks. Well, now your journey is over. Tonight you can see with your own eyes what language God speaks. He speaks the language of love, that is expressed in sharing, understanding, mercy, and total acceptance. Stay awhile and see if you experience any condemnation or rejection here. Be in touch with your heart, and check if there is any fear there. Relax, and know that you have found a safe place, where the language is so simple, and yet so real, that you could not possibly put it into words. Welcome, Emmanuel!'

Whatever title ends up on the cover of this book, I write the thoughts that come from my own reflections. I don't ever consider these, or want these to be anything profound! I do believe, however, that for those who have the luxury of time to be able to reflect on the 'sweet mysteries of life', and of God's entering into that journey, there is a veritable goldmine of inner nourishment and refreshment. Reflection is the nourishment of the soul. We live in a world where we can easily get caught up in the wall of fire, and it is only by speed that we can hope to avoid being trapped or losing momentum. Life can take over, we are no longer in control, and we end up with the proverbial situation, where the tail is wagging the dog. I remember coming across a book some years ago called 'Stop the world! I want to get off!' Bethlehem wasn't exactly the hub of the universe. God's ways are certainly not our ways. Life is fragile, handle with prayer! We are treading on a mine-field here. In no way should we venture out on our own. Jesus has come to join us on the journey. 'I will never abandon you. I will not leave you orphan. I will not abandon you in the storm. I will be with you always.' The problem with language is that it must be heard as well as spoken, whatever form that 'speaking' may take. I could fill several pages of this book with the promises of Jesus, but nothing I can do will lift those words off the page, and place them in a human heart.

There are so many possible approaches to all of this. I could ask myself what I want to hear, what I expect to hear, what I need to hear. If I gave the exact same message to six people right now, and sent them out to tell others, you'd be amazed what varied forms that message would assume over the next few hours! I spent many years as a teacher, and, if nothing else, it taught me that I can never presume that what I said was what was heard! When it comes to the language of God, I would sincerely suggest that the responsibility for both the speaking and the hearing be entrusted to God. It is said that the wise man practises what he preaches, and only the fool preaches what he practises! Over the years, before beginning a homily, I pray the Spirit of God to bless all of us, in the speaking and in the listening. The anointing must be on both sides, just as the responsibility is shared equally. I smile when I think of someone sitting back, wondering what Father X has to say today! God's problem could well be what Mr Y or Mrs Z is going to hear today! As I write, the television is the next room is a good example of what I have in mind here. If you were to look into that room now, there is nothing on the screen. This does not mean that there is nothing being transmitted at this time, nothing being said, nothing on line. It simply means that the television is not switched on. All the TV stations in the world can be spending millions at this very moment, but there is nothing reaching me until I press a button. Pressing that button is my decision, when it suits me, when I am ready, when I want to listen and see. Addiction to television must be a very tyrannical experience! I would just hate to be compelled to press that button!

Spirit and Breath of God, I often think of you as a telephone wire between God and me. Without you, there is no communication. Please continue to speak the language of God within my heart, to reveal that language to me, and to teach me its richness and its fulness. Speak, Lord, your servant is listening. Amen.

38. With the eyes of the world

In my younger, more ambitious and more enthusiastic days, I had a great desire to know all the available answers about God, religion, beliefs, and church. I would need all that to be able to answer all those people who were so ignorant as to even question such changeless, infallible truths! My strength and power, as a militant Christian, would come from books, and would be stored in my head, like an arsenal, until the attack had to be repelled! I smile now, when I think of this, and I accept that it's probably a normal mile-stone on most people's journey. I am also aware, of course, of a much greater sense of freedom, of a much lesser sense of responsibility. God is quite capable of defending himself! If he ever needs to use me as his spokesperson, he will supply the wisdom and the words. Jesus said 'My kingdom is not of this world.' Now that's not just a statement, that's a whole proclamation. If his kingdom is not of this world, then I shouldn't expect it to have any of the qualities of an earthly kingdom. It is not based on wealth, political clout, human wisdom, or social standing. In fact, it is a contradiction in itself to every quality a human kingdom might display. Scripture tells us that God actually chooses the weak as his most powerful instrument, because his power in more evident when seen in the lives of the weak. 'The kingdom, the power, and the glory are yours.' If I supply any of the power I could easily be tempted to steal some of the glory!

The church has always had to struggle to maintain its prophetic role, and its other-worldly values. It certainly didn't always succeed, either, and there is always need for on-going renewal. From away back in the time of Constantine, very early in the history of the church, the pollution began, when the spirit and values of the world began to seep into the life of the church. Constantine did nobody a favour, when he canonised Roman law, and Romanised Canon Law! It was as early as that the confusion entered in, and, before long, there was a levelling off between the two kingdoms, and the kingdom of Jesus Christ was highjacked by worldly influences. It was as early as then that bishops began living in palaces, and even the clothes, the thrones, the armies were common to both. This was a sad time, and we certainly have not fully recovered from it yet. However, there are signs, hopeful signs, and the church alignment with the oppressed and the poor is becoming more vocal and more evident. Many a church person has paid the supreme sacrifice for daring to confront the powers of this world with the errors of their ways. Prophets have often tended to end up as martyrs, because the world just cannot deal with the power of peaceful resistance of a Mahatma Ghandi or a Martin Luther King. The only way the world can deal with such is to kill them, forgetting, of course, that this does not silence their voices. The world thinks in straight lines, and everything has to make sense up in the head.

With a broad swipe at modern psychological testing and skill assessment, someone suggested that if Jesus had sent his twelve apostles for these tests, this well might have been the reply sent back to him:

'Thank you for submitting the resumes of the twelve men that you have picked for managerial positions in your new organisation. All of them have taken our battery of tests. We have run the results through our own computer, after having arranged personal interviews for each of them with our psychological and vocational aptitude consultant. It is generally agreed here that most of your nominees are lacking in background, education, and vocational aptitude for such an enterprise. They have no team concept, and their work experience in this field is non-existent.

Simon Peter is emotionally unstable, and given to fits of temper. Andrew has no leadership qualities. The two bothers, James and John, place personal interest above company loyalty. Thomas shows a sceptical attitude that would tend to undermine morale. Matthew has been black-listed by the Jerusalem Better Business Bureau for collecting taxes for foreigners. James, son of Alpheus, and Thaddeus definitely have radical leanings, and registered a high score on the manic-depressive scale.

One of the candidates, however, shows real potential. He is a man of ability and resourcefulness, meets people well, and has contacts in high places. He is highly motivated, ambitious, and responsible. We, therefore, recommend Judas Iscariot as your controller, and right-hand man!'

Once again I write with tongue in cheek, while, once again, saying that many a truth is spoken in jest. There is just no way that the world could possibly understand what Jesus was about. The stable was a non-runner, for starters! (I hope my horse-racing friends understand what it meant by that last remark!) The whole idea was crazy from the start, and the world has always tended to dismiss Jesus and his followers as dreamers or fools. The crown of thorns, and the mocking salutations typified all of that. Nothing much has changed since then. I must never forget, however, that, as a Christian, I owe nothing to this world. I don't need to justify my stands and my principles. Someone with a worldly mind-set wouldn't understand them, anyhow. St Paul reminds us that we are ambassadors for Christ. Now an ambassador is someone who represents a power that is based elsewhere. The ambassador is not an independent agent, and is continually in touch with base for instructions, advice, and directives. The ambassador has no power of her/his own, and is bound to reflect as accurately as possible the thinking, policies, and philosophies of the power being represented. In other words, I am certainly not alone, and I don't need to worry about what I should do or say. 'The Holy Spirit will give you a wisdom that no one will be able to oppose', says Jesus. An ambassador is never sent off somewhere, without contact, support, or directions. Ambassadors are transferred, and, sooner or later, are always recalled. My places of witness can vary, and the scope of that witness can change with age, or mobility. Eventually, of course, I will be recalled.

Even as a Christian, I need to remind myself of the central theme of Christ's kingdom. If I lose sight of that, I can easily get discouraged, because I can experience a sense of exile here, being surrounded by values contrary to my own. I need to remember that I am commissioned, I am sent, I have a very definite mandate. If the psychologists referred to above ran a battery of tests on me, I mightn't do much better that most of the apostles! However, that is not the yards-stick, and I do not have to measure up to the expectations of this world. I often joke that the most human people I know are the very young, and the very old. One group hasn't yet begun trying to impress others, and the second group are finished trying! We sometimes dismiss the latter group by referring to them as being in their second childhood. Jesus speaks of becoming like little children. This does not mean childishness but childlikeness. It is a freedom, among other things, from meeting the demands of this world, 'the freedom of the children of God.'

> *Lord Jesus, I was smiling as I wrote about the evaluation of your apostles! I honestly don't think, Lord, I would do any better than most, and I was glad about that! I certainly want to be available to you, and I open my heart and my whole being to you. Somehow, Lord, I believe that this is the test you apply. Thank you, Lord. Amen.*

39. Praying with the heart

At the time of writing I am living and working in a nursing home. There are full-time residents, and several others convalescing after surgery. Just this morning I spoke with a man recovering from a heart transplant operation. I was joking his wife as I said that it will be interesting to monitor his behaviour now, with his new heart. Will he be more kind-hearted, warm-hearted, soft-hearted?! As it happens, the man in question is a consummate gentleman, and always was. Therefore, it is reasonable to presume that he will continue to be so. When we speak of the heart, in terms of that part where I am my most authentic, the centre of my whole being, we are not, of course, referring to the physical. The body is not me. I am living in the body. At the core of my being (a word which comes from the Latin *cor*, meaning heart), there lives that part of me that is made directly in God's image and likeness. This is sometimes referred to as The Inner Child. This part of me continues to survive, no matter how much it is neglected or ignored. It never goes away, it never dies. Even when the body lies in the coffin, that part of me has gone ahead to the next and the final part of the journey. Inner peace, and inner wholeness come directly from proper attention being paid to that Inner Child. Like any child, there is a great fear of rejection, of hurt, of disowning. 'To thine own self be true, and then thou canst be false to any one.'

It is in this part of my Being that God's Spirit dwells. It can be a veritable Holy of Holies, a Pentecost Place, a Prayer Room. It is to this place that I should go in prayer. The organ God gave me to pray with is the heart, not the tongue. Sometimes I use the tongue to express the prayer that's in the heart. Scripture speaks of 'These people honour me with their lips, but their hearts are far from me' And the words of Jesus in the Temple could be applied to the human heart, if I allowed him enter there with a whip of cords 'My house shall be called a house of prayer, but you have made it a den of thieves.' Once again, we have another concept for prayer, where I can sit in some quiet place, go down into the heart, and then invite Jesus to enter there with that whip of cords. I can declare my willingness and my desire to renounce anything there that is not from him. It can, indeed, be a cleansing experience.

I conducted a funeral the other day. I asked the granddaughter of the woman who died to come up and speak to us about her. After all, she would know her much better than I did. Anyhow, she was shocked at first, and protested that she couldn't possibly do any such thing. I stuck with her, however, and, eventually, she came around to at least considering it. She asked for some directives, and I gave her one: 'Speak from the heart, and in that way you'll be sure to speak to the hearts of your listeners.' I was delighted for her that her words made a deep impression, and everybody was deeply moved. The very same secret applies to every talk I ever give, to every letter I ever write, to every word I ever speak.

A man died recently, and went to heaven. He was very happy about the whole thing, and, after a few days, he began to wander about, exploring, to see all that was to be seen. He was out on such a venture when he chanced to bump into Jesus, and he expressed his joy, and his gratitude. This was away so much more than he had ever hoped for, from below. He spoke of the vast gap he now realised existed between this stage and the one he had just left. Jesus listened with great love, interest, and patience. Jesus also questioned just whether that gap was as vast as appeared. To make things clearer, the Lord offered him a little experiment.

He opened up a trap-door in the floor of heaven. From there they both could see this man's local church, on this Sunday Morning, while a Mass was in progress. The man could see all the people, the priest, the Mass servers, the readers, the choir. There was great movement of hands, lips, and heads, but he was really puzzled, because he couldn't hear a sound. He could see the priest and the people turning over pages in the missalette. He could see the choir turning pages in their hymnals. He could see the organist pounding away at the keyboard. But he still couldn't hear any sound. This puzzled him greatly. He turned to

Jesus for an explanation, and, before he had the question out of his mouth, Jesus looked at him, and with total sincerity, whispered 'We have a rule here. It has always been here, and it always will. If those people down there don't speak, pray, or sing with their hearts, we cannot hear a sound up here.'

Prayer can be as simple and as easy as I allow it to be. It is about quality, never about quantity. The Lord weighs my prayers, rather than counts them. God's Spirit is a Spirit of truth. That is central to any possible understanding of this. If God's Spirit is present, it is prayer, if not, it is human endeavour, where I'm only talking to myself. Now if God's Spirit is present, the whole thing must be based on truth, sincerity, authenticity. God would never be involved in anything less. That is why the heart must be involved in all my dealings with God. Scripture speaks of repentance in these words 'I will remove your heart of stone, and give you a heart of flesh. I will give you a new heart, and I will put my Spirit within you.' From a very early age I learned that I was to love the Lord, my God, with all my heart ...'. I didn't then, of course, understand this, but it's beginning to make some sense to me now. The all-my-heart part is not something that I can determine or quantify. I leave that entirely to God. I open the doors and invite him enter, and if he wants part, half, or all, he is welcome! I would be afraid to have this determination within my power and control, because human nature can be very devious! I answer the door where there is a beggar-woman, and I decide to give her something. No matter how generous I may feel, I will take control of the giving. I will give what I decide. I'm not likely to walk out the door, invite her to enter, and help herself! There is nothing wrong with this, of course, but it becomes a problem when I behave in this way with the Lord. God loves me, and everything he does with me, for me, in me, is totally motivated by what is for my good. St John says 'If we do not trust him, it shows that we are afraid of what he might do to us. And if we are afraid of what he might do to us, it shows that we are not yet fully convinced that he really loves us.' Once again, we come to that bottom line, where we are faced with whether we are convinced of his love. How wise it is to say that the saint is not the person who loves God. Rather is it the person who is totally convinced that God loves her/him.

'Create in me a new heart, and put a steadfast spirit within me' is the prayer of the Psalmist. If the heart is re-created, the whole person is renewed. Jesus says that what comes out of a person is what makes a person good or bad. The heart can be full of deceit, and so the words and actions are impregnated with that spirit. It is a beautiful, simple, and wonderful thought that God should be in control of the heart. As with the man in our story, if the heart is praying, the gap between here and heaven is totally bridged.

Spirit and Breath of God, source of all prayer, fill my heart, and flood my whole being with a song of praise and a prayer of thanks. Please lift my spirits out of the quicksand of selfishness, and the stagnant pools of indifference. Put a song of praise in my heart before it reaches my lips. Amen.

40. Completing the work

In Eucharistic Prayer IV, we have the following words 'And that we might live no longer for ourselves, but for him, he sent his Holy Spirit, as his first gift to those who believe, to complete his work on earth, and to bring us the fulness of grace'. It is important that we always remember that it is his work. He began it, and he will see it to completion, except that he wishes to involve us in that completion. I shouldn't ever think that God needs me! He needs me only in that he needs people to love, because love isn't love until it is given away. When Jesus came that first Christmas night, he set the process in motion. He will come at the end to close down the shop, to tie up the loose ends, and to put the final touch of approval to his victory, in the establishing of his one and eternal kingdom. In the meantime, the work of building up that kingdom must continue, and every one of us has a part to play in that work. At the end of the last war, there was a surrender, and a cease-fire. However, in many parts of the Far East, the 'mopping up' continued for some time. The war was, effectively, over, but there were still many pockets of resistance that still needed to be flushed out. Even years later, it was known that there were soldiers in the jungles, who either didn't know that the war was over, or who refused to accept that fact. As Christians, we know that Jesus has the victory, but that victory needs to be proclaimed and consolidated.

The first place I need to proclaim and consolidate that victory is within my own heart, and in my own life. In recent years, we have witnessed the return of the various ministries of the laity. Being a Lector is one such ministry, which involves reading at Mass. To exercise such a ministry involves much more than just being able to read. In the old days, when an attacker was repulsed, after invading a country, and was driven back over the border, heralds were sent from place to place to proclaim that victory. The people were gathered together, and, in a loud and clear voice, the herald proclaimed that the enemy had been defeated, and the victory had been achieved. The reader at Mass is proclaiming good news, and the listeners need to hear the word as a proclamation of good news. This proclaiming is central to missionary endeavour, and to all forms of evangelisation. Jesus gains the victory, but he needs us to proclaim it. The work is not complete if people haven' t heard it. And, as St Paul says 'How will they know, if no one tells them, and how will they be told, if no one is sent?'

My vocation as a priest is not to save souls. My vocation is to tell people that they are already saved. When this has been done, there remains one last step. Those who know they are saved, have to ensure that they look saved, otherwise there is no witness. The fact that Jesus rose from the dead is, of course, a victory. He then needs people, however, who are his witnesses to the resurrection. In their lives must be the evidence of the victory over sin, sickness, and death. Each one is living flesh-and-blood proof of that victory. Jesus is the Light who came into a world of darkness, and each of us is a candle, lit from that light, so that the light is carried to every corner of darkness. 'Let your light shine before people, that they may see your good works, and glorify your Father in heaven.' It is much better to light a candle than curse the darkness. One candle is sufficient to dispel the darkness in a whole room. Like the athlete carrying the Olympic torch, each of us is a light-bearer, each of us carries the light of Christ, until the whole world has been cleared of darkness.

Puccini wrote *La Boheme* and *Madame Butterfly*. It was during his battle with terminal cancer in 1922 that he began to write *Turandoe*, which many now consider his best. He worked on the score, day and night, despite the advice of friends to rest, and to save his energy. When his sickness worsened, Puccini said to his pupils, 'If I don't finish *Turandoe*, I want you to finish it.' He died in 1924, and left the work unfinished.

His pupils gathered all that was written of *Turandoe*, studied it in great detail, and then proceeded to write the remainder of the opera. The world premiere was performed in the La Scala Opera House in Milan in 1926, and it was conducted by Toscanini,

Puccini's favourite student. The opera went beautifully until Toscanini came to the end of the part written personally by Puccini. He stopped the music, put down the baton, turned to the audience, and announced, 'Thus far the master wrote, but he died.'

There was a long pause. No one moved. Then Toscanini picked up the baton, turned to the audience, and, with tears in his eyes, announced 'But his disciples finished his work.' The opera closed to thunderous applause, and to a permanent place in the annals of great works.

It is reckoned today that it is almost impossible to distinguish where exactly Puccini stopped composing, and his pupils took over. It is interesting to notice that, before they dared write a note, they had to study what the master had written up till then. They had to enter into the mind, heart, and vision of the composer, to capture his spirit, and to maintain the direction he had taken. They had to allow Puccini to continue to guide the composition, because, after all, it was his work. Their privilege was just to complete something that had been set in motion in such a way that it now had a life of its own. Their responsibility was to nurture, nurse, and guide it towards its logical conclusion. It is absolutely essential for us, as Christians, to saturate ourselves in the thinking and the teaching of Jesus. We are called to make ourselves available to the Holy Spirit, who came to complete the score. This is more serious, and much more important than a piece of music. This has eternal ramifications, effecting the whole world, and effecting our eternal salvation. This is why the Holy Spirit takes over the completion of Jesus' work, because it would be an impossible task for mere humans. It is, of course, a wonderful, exciting, and extraordinary calling, and happy indeed are they who hear that call. A spirit of any kind cannot do anything of itself. An evil spirit needs a hand to plant the bomb, a mind to conceive the evil, a tongue to tell the lie. It is the same with the Holy Spirit, who enables things get done, who provides the power to get things done, and who inspires the doing of things. It is we, however, who have to do the things. The Holy Spirit needs our hands, feet, and voice. He needs, ideally, that we make ourselves totally available to him. The more available I am, of course, the greater the Spirit can work through me. It is not for me to quantify this, because I don't honestly think I can. In others words, I can never say 'now today, I will make two-thirds of myself available' ! I believe all I can do is open my heart, and, day after day, invite the Spirit to take over there. I may, and probably will, get constant evidence, that there's still alot of unclaimed wilderness within me, but not to fear. The Spirit works at whatever pace is best for my good. Because we are speaking of the power of God here, the Spirit, of course, is even able to use my very weaknesses for good. Not every note of the score gets equal length or equal stress. It is in the harmony of everything that the music is.

Lord Jesus, thank you for calling me to be an instrument through which you continue your work here on earth. Please never allow me forget the privilege, or take that call for granted. I know only too well that I do not deserve this, and that I am very unworthy. However, thanks to your Spirit, I can accept the fact that I have, indeed, been chosen, appointed, anointed, and commissioned. Thank you, Lord. Amen.

Thematic Index

Numbers refer to the story numbers

Attitude 10, 21, 33, 38, 39.
Baptism 3, 10, 12, 34.
Children 7, 8, 9, 10, 11, 12, 14, 16, 17, 22, 24, 35, 37.
Christian 3, 10, 12, 14, 23, 26, 27, 34, 38, 39, 40.
Christmas 2, 29, 37.
Community 10, 12, 14, 34.
Conversion 13, 21, 23, 30, 38.
Death 1, 7, 18, 19, 23.
Decision 21, 26, 28, 31.
Despair 4, 21, 23, 32, 37..
Example 3, 7, 9, 21, 22, 24, 37.
Faith 1, 23, 35, 37.
Family 3, 7, 8, 9, 10, 11, 12, 14, 16, 22, 25, 30, 35.
Father's Love 8, 9, 22, 23, 35.
Forgiveness 5, 30, 35, 37.
Gift 17, 25.
Heart 7, 13, 16, 24, 31, 32, 38.
Heaven 2, 17, 23.
Holy Spirit 13, 24, 25, 33.
Hope 21, 23, 32, 37.
Jesus 2, 5, 10, 11, 23, 26, 31, 37, 40.
Lies 15, 22, 23, 33, 36, 38.
Love 7, 8, 9, 12, 16, 29, 30, 31, 71.
Marriage 12, 29.
Mothers 12, 14, 16, 17, 24.
New Life 13, 19, 24.
Prayer 20, 32, 39.
Religion 10, 12, 31, 32, 33.
Salvation 5, 11, 17, 23, 37.
Satan 15, 28.
Service 9, 18, 27, 29, 34, 40.
Sin 4, 5, 6, 23, 30, 36.
Trust 1, 20, 21, 32, 35.
Truth 4, 6, 12, 22, 23, 32, 33, 38.
World 36, 38.